2003

Medical Ethics

Other Books in the Current Controversies Series:

The Abortion Controversy
Alcoholism
Assisted Suicide
Capital Punishment
Computers and Society
Conserving the Environment
Crime
The Disabled
Drug Trafficking
Ethics
Europe
Family Violence
Free Speech
Gambling
Garbage and Waste
Gay Rights
Genetics and Intelligence
Gun Control
Guns and Violence
Hate Crimes
Hunger
Illegal Drugs
Illegal Immigration

The Information Highway
Interventionism
Iraq
Marriage and Divorce
Mental Health
Minorities
Nationalism and Ethnic
    Conflict
Native American Rights
Police Brutality
Politicians and Ethics
Pollution
Prisons
Racism
Reproductive Technologies
The Rights of Animals
Sexual Harassment
Smoking
Teen Addiction
Urban Terrorism
Violence Against Women
Violence in the Media
Women in the Military

Medical Ethics

James D. Torr, *Book Editor*

David Bender, *Publisher*
Bruno Leone, *Executive Editor*

Bonnie Szumski, *Editorial Director*
David M. Haugen, *Managing Editor*

CURRENT CONTROVERSIES

Cover photo: © Larry Mulvehill/Science Source/Photo Researchers

Library of Congress Cataloging-in-Publication Data

Medical ethics / James D. Torr, book editor.
        p. cm. — (Current controversies)
    Includes bibliographical references and index.
    ISBN 0-7377-0144-7 (pbk. : alk. paper). — ISBN 0-7377-0145-5
(lib. : alk. paper)
    1. Medical ethics Miscellanea. I. Torr, James D., 1974–   .
II. Series.
R724.M29273   2000
172'.4—dc21   99-34501
                                                                    CIP

©2000 by Greenhaven Press, Inc., PO Box 289009, San Diego, CA 92198-9009
Printed in the U.S.A.

Contents

Foreword   11

Introduction   13

Chapter 1: Should Physicians Ever Hasten Patients' Deaths?

Prolonging Life and Death: An Overview *by Robert B. Mellert*   17
Two different approaches to medical ethics often shape discussions about end-of-life decision making. The traditional "curing" approach argues that the purpose of medicine is to heal and preserve life. In this view, any action that hastens a patient's death is contrary to the goals of medicine. The "caring" approach, on the other hand, emphasizes that physicians should work to minimize pain and that, above all, they should respect the wishes of their patients, even when patients wish to die.

Yes: Physicians Should Sometimes Hasten Patients' Deaths

Physicians Should Not Provide Futile Treatment
by Nancy S. Jecker and Lawrence J. Schneiderman   24
Physicians should not provide treatments that have a very low chance of succeeding or that do not provide any real benefit to a patient, such as artificial respirators for patients in a permanent vegetative state. Such treatments are medically futile and physicians have no obligation to provide them, even when patients or their family members request that doctors "do everything possible" to prolong life.

Physician-Assisted Suicide Is Consistent with Medical Ethics
by Timothy E. Quill, Lonny J. Shavelson, and Fred S. Marcus   31
Physicians have a responsibility to preserve life, but they also have a duty to relieve human suffering. Physician-assisted suicide is consistent with medical ethics when a patient's suffering becomes extreme and he or she clearly and repeatedly requests assistance in hastening death. Under these circumstances, relieving suffering is more important than prolonging life for a few more days or weeks.

Physicians Should Be Permitted to Assist in Suicide *by Marcia Angell*   33
It should not be a crime for doctors to respect the wishes of terminally ill, mentally competent patients who want assistance in committing suicide. Decisions about how to die are personal, private matters that the government should stay out of. Dying patients have the right to choose a quick, painless death, and doctors should be allowed to help them achieve it.

No: Physicians Should Never Hasten Patients' Deaths

Physicians Should Not Withhold Lifesaving Treatments
by Wesley J. Smith   36

In many hospitals around the country, doctors are refusing to treat co-
matose and brain-damaged patients on the grounds that such patients
would be better off dead. The law surrounding such cases is unclear, but
courts are increasingly willing to side with doctors and hospitals rather
than patients' families. Futile-care policies are part of a larger movement
toward health care rationing, in which physicians and bioethicists will decide who is worthy and who is unworthy of being kept alive.

Physician-Assisted Suicide Violates Medical Ethics *by Daniel Callahan*   42

A physician who participates in another person's suicide abuses medici-
nal principles. Doctors should do everything in their power to relieve suffering, but must never seek to cause death, whether directly or indirectly.
Physicians must limit themselves to the promotion and preservation of
health, and resist the temptation to believe that medicine can solve the
eternal, unavoidable problems of suffering and death.

Physicians Should Not Be Permitted to Assist in Suicide
by Rita L. Marker   45

Physician-assisted suicide is often touted as an option that doctors and patients should only consider as a last resort. In reality, however, doctors
and hospitals have financial incentives to keep costs down, and assisted
suicide is the least expensive way to deal with patients who require expensive treatment. Thus, if assisted suicide becomes legal, it will quickly
become the only option most Americans can afford, since health insurance companies often refuse to cover expensive end-of-life care.

Chapter 2: What Ethics Should Guide Organ Transplants?

The Ethics of Organ Transplants: An Overview *by Karen K. Giuliano*   51

Organ transplants are a continual problem for the medical community because the number of people waiting for a lifesaving transplant far exceeds
the number of organs donated each year. Deciding who will receive these
scarce organs is literally a life-and-death decision for the patients involved. The only way to alleviate the problems of organ allocation is to
increase the number of organs available for transplant. Some people advocate providing financial incentives for people to donate, while others
believe the shortage in organs can be solved by the use of animal-to-
human transplants—but both of these approaches raise ethical questions
of their own.

Animal-to-Human Transplants Could Save Lives
by David White, interviewed by Cory SerVaas   57

Scientists are close to perfecting techniques that will allow pig organs to
be transplanted safely into humans. The use of pig-to-human transplants
will save the lives of the thousands of people who currently die each year
because of the shortage of human organ donors.

Animal-to-Human Transplants Are Dangerous and Unethical
by Alan Berger and Gil Lamont   61
  Animal-to-human transplants are incredibly dangerous because they provide a means for animal viruses to spread among the human population.
  Nevertheless, the government is promoting expensive, unsafe animal-to-
  human transplants. Even if the inherent dangers of animal-to-human
  transplants can be overcome, sacrificing animals in order to save humans
  is unethical. A better way to deal with the organ shortage is to encourage
  more people to donate and to educate Americans about healthy lifestyles,
  so that fewer people will need transplants at all.

Commerce in Organs Is Ethical *by Leonard Lu*   67
  Allowing individuals to sell their spare kidney would benefit both the
  seller, who would make money from the transaction, and the buyer,
  whose life would be saved. The donor of an organ should be able to profit
  from the transplant procedure just as doctors and drug companies do.
  Kidney removal is a somewhat risky procedure, but society permits
  people to profit from far more dangerous ventures, such as coal mining
  and test piloting. Commerce in human organs can be consistent with medical ethics if the practice is strictly regulated to prevent abuse.

Commerce in Organs Is Unethical *by Stephen G. Post*   73
  The buying and selling of human organs violates human dignity and results in the oppression of the poor. The libertarian idea that the human
  body is merely property that can be sold off is objectionable. Commerce
  in human organs will undercut the spirit of philanthropy that currently
  drives organ donation, and this may actually decrease supply.

Commerce in Organs Could Save Lives *by Pete du Pont*   77
  Organs for transplantation are in short supply because it is illegal for individuals to receive any type of compensation for the organs they donate.
  Providing incentives for donation, including paying people for their organs, would increase the supply of organs, and fewer people would die
  while waiting for transplants.

Commerce in Organs Has Led to Human Rights Violations   80
by David J. Rothman
  The worldwide demand for lifesaving organ transplants, coupled with the
  insufficient number of organs donated each year, has created an international black market for human organs. In India poor villagers sell their
  kidneys to wealthy foreigners, and in China, the organs of executed
  prisoners are harvested and sold for profit. Medical organizations must
  oppose these gross violations of human rights.

Chapter 3: Are Reproductive Technologies Ethical?

Reproductive Technologies: An Overview *by Karen Wright*   88
  Since 1978, when the first test-tube baby was born, the use of reproductive
  technologies to overcome fertility has risen steadily. Fertility drugs, in vitro
  fertilization, and surrogate motherhood have enabled thousands of infertile
  couples to reproduce, and some scientists are even discussing the possibility of using cloning technology to produce a child that is genetically identical to one of its parents. These new procedures have raised a host of ethical
  questions relating to the use of technology to help create life.

Yes: Reproductive Technologies Are Ethical

Reproductive Technologies Are a Valid Medical Treatment
by Diane D. Aronson   97

Infertility is a disability, and assisted reproductive technologies are a valid medical treatment for this disability. Having children and building a family is an important life goal, and couples who need medical assistance to achieve this goal should receive it. Health insurance should provide coverage for infertility treatments just as it does for other types of disability.

Reproductive Technologies Can Be Consistent with Christian Beliefs
by Elvonne Whitney   102

Although assisted reproduction does raise many ethical questions, biblical principles can help guide Christians in the proper use of reproductive technologies. In the Bible there are instances in which God miraculously blesses couples with pregnancy; reproductive technologies are simply a more mundane way that God helps couples to overcome infertility.

Multiple Births Are an Acceptable Consequence of Assisted Reproduction *by Marianne Moody Jennings*   106

The parents of the McCaughey septuplets and Chuckwu octuplets should not be criticized for their use of reproductive technologies. Multiple pregnancies resulting from these technologies are rare, but even when they do occur they are often viewed as a blessing by the couple that is trying to start a family. Some medical ethicists and media pundits have condemned multiple births as unwise and irresponsible, but their criticisms are exaggerated, unwarranted, and inappropriate.

Cloning Can Be an Acceptable Means of Reproduction
by James Q. Wilson   109

Many people are repulsed by the idea of cloning human beings, but the benefits of cloning as a means of reproduction may outweigh the risks. There are many risks associated with permitting the cloning of human beings, but these are chiefly associated with the potential to create children who have no parents. If cloning human beings becomes technologically possible, it should only be available to married couples who are unable to reproduce by other means.

No: Reproductive Technologies Are Unethical

Reproductive Technologies Are Morally Problematic
by Jacqueline Laing   116

Reproductive technologies have raised a host of moral problems that have yet to be addressed. The doctors involved in assisted reproduction treat procreation as a manufacturing process and children as commodities. These fertility specialists must stop viewing themselves merely as technologists and realize that their actions have profound consequences for the children they help create.

Some Reproductive Technologies Violate Christian Beliefs
by Daniel McConchie   120

Christians must be wary of the ethical dilemmas that surround assisted reproduction. Fertility drugs and in vitro fertilization must be used wisely to avoid creating unwanted embryos that might be later discarded, or, in the case of multiple pregnancies, aborted. Surrogate motherhood and the use of donated sperm or eggs have harmful consequences and should be avoided. Given the high costs and risks associated with reproductive technologies, adoption is often a more prudent choice for infertile couples who want to start a family.

Multiple Births Are a Harmful Consequence of Assisted Reproduction
by Ezekiel J. Emanuel   124
The births of the McCaughey septuplets and Chukwu octuplets have been glorified by the media, but in reality such multiple births are a very undesirable result of the misuse of fertility treatments. By carrying multiple pregnancies to term, parents risk all the fetuses' health. The children of multiple births experience long-term physical complications and receive far less individual attention from their parents. The standard of medical care should be to prevent such multiple pregnancies from happening, and, when they do, to reduce the number of fetuses through abortion.

Cloning Is Not an Acceptable Means of Reproduction by Commonweal   129
Human cloning is an unethical means of reproduction. Allowing someone to determine the entire genetic makeup of another person violates that person's individuality and dignity. Human cloning would play havoc with traditional notions of parenting and kinship, allowing mothers to give birth to their own genetic twins. Infertility is an unfortunate problem for many couples, but the desire to have a child does not justify such an inappropriate use of science and technology.

Chapter 4: What Ethics Should Guide Biomedical Research?

Stem Cell Research and Human Cloning: An Overview
by Gregg Easterbrook   133
Research involving stem cells—certain cells found in human embryos that can develop into any organ or tissue in the body—has the potential to cure many diseases by allowing physicians to replace failing cells with brand new body tissue. A major ethical problem with this research, however, is that stem cells must be taken from aborted fetuses or from test-tube embryos. Another disquieting aspect of stem cell research is that the same techniques used to manipulate stem cells in the lab could someday be used to clone human beings.

Research on Human Embryos Is Unethical by John J. Miller   143
Officials at the National Institutes of Health are trying to circumvent a congressional ban on federally-funded research involving human stem cells, claiming such research could help cure some diseases. However, this type of research is unethical because stem cells must be obtained either from aborted fetuses or from embryos that have been created through in vitro fertilization and then killed. Research that involves the destruction of human life is highly immoral; that is why the congressional ban was instituted in the first place.

Research on Human Embryos Can Be Ethical by Arthur Caplan   147
The moral problems inherent in human embryo research must be weighed against the enormous benefits such research may produce. Creating hu-

man embryos just so that they will be destroyed shows a disrespect for human life. However, when couples use in vitro fertilization to try to have a child, fertility specialists routinely create more embryos than the couple is likely to use. Across the country, thousands of spare embryos are being stored in the freezers of private fertility clinics. Using these embryos for research is ethically acceptable, since the only real alternative is to destroy them.

Research into Human Cloning Should Be Banned *by William Keeler*   153
Persons brought into the world through cloning would be viewed as manufactured people, mere copies of an original and hence inferior. This discriminatory view is already evident in some researchers' proposals that although research on human embryos is unethical, destroying *cloned* human embryos for research is acceptable. A ban on research into human cloning is necessary to prevent the creation of a new class of oppressed humans.

Research into Human Cloning Should Not Be Banned
by Ronald Bailey   158
Several politicians and bioethicists have rushed to ban human cloning, but their gory predictions that clones would be grown for their organs or trained to be carbon copies of their predecessors are unrealistic. Human clones would be no different than identical twins, so there is no reason to think that they would be treated as anything less than human beings. Unfounded fears about how cloning *might* be abused are an inadequate justification to outlaw such a promising field of research.

Bibliography   164
Organizations to Contact   167
Index   171

Foreword

By definition, controversies are "discussions of questions in which opposing opinions clash" (Webster's Twentieth Century Dictionary Unabridged). Few would deny that controversies are a pervasive part of the human condition and exist on virtually every level of human enterprise. Controversies transpire between individuals and among groups, within nations and between nations. Controversies supply the grist necessary for progress by providing challenges and challengers to the status quo. They also create atmospheres where strife and warfare can flourish. A world without controversies would be a peaceful world; but it also would be, by and large, static and prosaic.

The Series' Purpose

The purpose of the Current Controversies series is to explore many of the social, political, and economic controversies dominating the national and international scenes today. Titles selected for inclusion in the series are highly focused and specific. For example, from the larger category of criminal justice, Current Controversies deals with specific topics such as police brutality, gun control, white collar crime, and others. The debates in Current Controversies also are presented in a useful, timeless fashion. Articles and book excerpts included in each title are selected if they contribute valuable, long-range ideas to the overall debate. And wherever possible, current information is enhanced with historical documents and other relevant materials. Thus, while individual titles are current in focus, every effort is made to ensure that they will not become quickly outdated. Books in the Current Controversies series will remain important resources for librarians, teachers, and students for many years.

In addition to keeping the titles focused and specific, great care is taken in the editorial format of each book in the series. Book introductions and chapter prefaces are offered to provide background material for readers. Chapters are organized around several key questions that are answered with diverse opinions representing all points on the political spectrum. Materials in each chapter include opinions in which authors clearly disagree as well as alternative opinions in which authors may agree on a broader issue but disagree on the possible solutions. In this way, the content of each volume in Current Controversies mirrors the mosaic of opinions encountered in society. Readers will quickly realize that there are many viable answers to these complex issues. By questioning each author's conclusions, students and casual readers can begin to develop the critical thinking skills so important to evaluating opinionated material.

Current Controversies is also ideal for controlled research. Each anthology in the series is composed of primary sources taken from a wide gamut of informational categories including periodicals, newspapers, books, United States and foreign government documents, and the publications of private and public organizations. Readers will find factual support for reports, debates, and research papers covering all areas of important issues. In addition, an annotated table of contents, an index, a book and periodical bibliography, and a list of organizations to contact are included in each book to expedite further research.

Perhaps more than ever before in history, people are confronted with diverse and contradictory information. During the Persian Gulf War, for example, the public was not only treated to minute-to-minute coverage of the war, it was also inundated with critiques of the coverage and countless analyses of the factors motivating U.S. involvement. Being able to sort through the plethora of opinions accompanying today's major issues, and to draw one's own conclusions, can be a complicated and frustrating struggle. It is the editors' hope that Current Controversies will help readers with this struggle.

Greenhaven Press anthologies primarily consist of previously published material taken from a variety of sources, including periodicals, books, scholarly journals, newspapers, government documents, and position papers from private and public organizations. These original sources are often edited for length and to ensure their accessibility for a young adult audience. The anthology editors also change the original titles of these works in order to clearly present the main thesis of each viewpoint and to explicitly indicate the opinion presented in the viewpoint. These alterations are made in consideration of both the reading and comprehension levels of a young adult audience. Every effort is made to ensure that Greenhaven Press accurately reflects the original intent of the authors included in this anthology.

"Advances in medical technology are constantly expanding the scope of what medicine can accomplish; the purpose of medical ethics is to determine what medicine should *accomplish."*

Introduction

Physicians have always been confronted with life-and-death choices—having to make difficult decisions is part of the responsibility of being a doctor. But the predicaments that doctors find themselves in today are the subject of more interest and controversy than ever before, simply because advances in modern medicine over the past few decades have given rise to situations that no one would have expected in an earlier era.

Consider this scenario: A woman, heartbroken over her husband's death, chooses to have his memory live on in the form of a son. She pays to have fertility doctors, using cloning techniques and in vitro fertilization, impregnate her with an embryonic clone of her deceased husband. She gives birth to his genetic twin nine months later. Should fertility doctors be allowed to offer this type of service?

This scenario, of course, is entirely hypothetical. Scientists are not able to clone human beings—yet. In February 1997, researchers in Scotland announced that they had cloned a sheep they named Dolly. Another lab has reported success in cloning mice. But scientists do not currently have the capability to clone humans. Nevertheless, Richard Seed, a retired physicist, announced in January 1998 that he intends to set up a clinic to clone humans. He estimates that as many as 10,000 infertile couples would be interested in cloning themselves as a way of having children. If scientists can clone humans, they will probably also be able to clone persons who have recently died. So the ethical ramifications of the above scenario are worth considering. Would cloning a child or spouse who has recently died be ethical? What kind of life could the cloned child expect to have? Would the government be justified in outlawing such a practice?

Human cloning may seem like the stuff of science fiction. But then again, the idea that conception could take place outside the womb—through the now common procedure of in-vitro fertilization—also once struck people as fantastic. The birth of the first test-tube baby, Louise Brown, in 1978, shocked the nation. Physicians, ethicists, and religious leaders immediately questioned whether it was morally acceptable to use technology to help create life. Other advances in reproductive technology—sperm and egg donation, the freezing of human embryos, and the ability to implant only those embryos that have the most desirable genetic traits—have contributed to this unease, and the ethics of reproductive technologies are still hotly debated today, even as more and more couples turn to these techniques in the hopes of having a child.

The history of organ transplants also demonstrates how quickly controversial medical procedures can move from theory to reality. The notion that doctors could take organs from one body—either a corpse or a living donor—and transplant them into someone else once struck many people as ludicrous, even repugnant. Yet, in a relatively short time (organ transplants have been a common medical procedure only since 1983, when the immunosuppressant drug cyclosporin was developed) most people have come to view organ transplants as medical marvels that have saved thousands of lives rather than as something out of *Frankenstein*.

However, the ethical issues surrounding transplant technology have certainly not been fully resolved. For example, in 1990, human rights advocates were horrified to learn that in 1984, shortly after the development of cyclosporin, the Chinese government legalized the harvesting of organs from the bodies of executed prisoners. Many condemned the practice on the grounds that prison officials do not obtain the prisoner's consent to donate organs, and that the Chinese government illegally sells the organs for profit. Yet some argued that as long as the prisoners were going to die anyway, their organs might as well be used to save others. Thus, while organ transplants have saved thousands of lives, they have raised moral questions involving the use of the dead in order to help the living. This problem—that lifesaving technologies can easily be abused—is a common theme in medical ethics.

In addition to creating new problems for medical ethicists, medical advances may also exacerbate ones that already exist, such as the ages-old dilemma of when, if ever, a doctor should acknowledge that a patient has been lost to death. Suffering patients who sincerely wish to die have always been a problem for doctors, who must choose whether to respect the patient's wishes or to follow their own professional obligation to preserve life. Yet the euthanasia debate did not become a major issue in America until the 1970s, when it became clear that artificial respirators and other technologies could prolong a person's bodily existence even after his or her mind had ceased to function.

Faced with these medical advances, many people said they would rather die than risk being hooked up to a machine. Doctors were forced to debate whether ending a patient's life was ever the right thing to do, and this debate continues today. In November 1997, Oregon legalized physician-assisted suicide, but only for terminally ill patients. Then, in 1999, the notorious euthanasia doctor Jack Kevorkian received a twenty-five-year prison sentence for administering a lethal injection to a terminally ill patient who asked for help in ending his life. These seemingly contradictory developments indicate that while some Americans will accept physician-assisted suicide if it is strictly regulated, as in Oregon, most fear putting too much power over death in the hands of doctors.

Much like organ transplants, physician-assisted suicide is a procedure that some people regard as beneficial, but that can easily lead to abuse.

Advances in medical technology are constantly expanding the scope of what medicine can accomplish; the purpose of medical ethics is to determine what medicine *should* accomplish. The question facing many doctors and patients is whether medical ethics can keep up with the rapid pace of technology. Arthur Caplan, head of the Center for Bioethics at the University of Pennsylvania, believes they can. "Medicine and science do move quickly," he writes in his book, *Moral Matters: Ethical Issues in Medicine and the Life Sciences*, and he stresses the need for doctors and ethicists to constantly evaluate new medical technologies to ensure that they are used in morally appropriate ways. But he rejects the idea that biotechnology is out of control: "The only reason medicine and science can leap ahead of our ethics is if we choose to allow that to happen." Others believe that recent developments in medicine are cause for alarm. "In little more than a generation, our definition of life and the meaning of existence is likely to be radically altered," writes Jeremy Rifkin, a prominent opponent of cloning and genetic engineering, "Our very sense of self and society will likely change during what I call the emerging Biotech Century." The authors in *Medical Ethics: Current Controversies* debate the changing world of medical ethics in the following chapters: Should Physicians Ever Hasten Patients' Deaths? What Ethics Should Guide Organ Transplants? Are Reproductive Technologies Ethical? What Ethics Should Guide Biomedical Research?

Chapter 1

Should Physicians Ever Hasten Patients' Deaths?

Prolonging Life and Death: An Overview

by Robert B. Mellert

About the author: *Robert B. Mellert is a professor of philosophy and religious studies at Brookdale Community College in Lincroft, New Jersey, and the author of* Seven Ethical Theories.

Deciding when to live and when to die is an issue that has only recently begun to confront the human species. It is a difficult decision, and we are not yet skilled in making it. Today, doctors and patients are increasingly being forced to make these life and death—and *quality* of life and death—decisions amid rapid technological change, startling new medical discoveries, an aggressively litigious society, and sharply disagreeing medical ethicists.

Discussion on medical ethics now involves two competing theories about the nature of health care. One is the "curing" approach, based upon traditional medical ethical principles that go back as far as the Hippocratic oath. These principles have been neatly formulated into a list of standards that can be found in just about every textbook in medical ethics: the principle of life, the principle of beneficence, the principle of nonmaleficence, and the principle of justice.

The second approach, "caring," focuses on patient autonomy, proper "bedside manners" by health-care providers, preparation of living wills, and the hospice movement. The concerns represented by this approach have, of course, always been present in medical assistance, but their emergence as a primary focus of medicine is more recent.

The Curing Tradition

The "curing" approach to medical ethics argues that the role of medicine is to heal. This objective is in harmony with the person's right to life. To subordinate healing to some other function, such as caring, would violate the nature of medicine itself. Caring, of course, is important, but it must only be seen as subservient to the primary task of curing.

Traditional Western religious ethics can be used to support the curing ap-

Reprinted from Robert B. Mellert, "Cure or Care: The Future of Medical Ethics," *The Futurist,* July/August 1997, with permission from The World Future Society, 7910 Woodmont Ave., Bethesda, MD 20814.

proach. The sanctity of human life is an important ideal in this morality. Because it is a gift from God, life must be sustained to the extent reasonably possible, and all ordinary measures must be taken to preserve it. This tradition holds that only God's authority can decide the time of death. Even if a dying patient is suffering, the job of the health professional must never include options such as assisted suicide, or even medication that would shorten life.

> *"The 'curing' approach to medical ethics argues that the role of medicine is to heal."*

In the curing approach, physicians are the primary decision makers. What to do in order to preserve life is primarily a medical judgment. As professionals who are knowledgeable about the relevant medical procedures and who are best able to judge their efficacy, physicians can expect patients to trust them and accept their recommendations. The physician explains to the patient why specific procedures are recommended in the given circumstances, and then the patient consents. This model of the doctor-patient relationship is often called the paternalistic model.

The Caring Approach

The second approach to medical ethics, "caring," is more utilitarian or situational. Jeremy Bentham, the nineteenth-century British philosopher, perhaps best expresses the utilitarian standard as "the maximization of pleasure and the minimization of pain." This standard is justified on the grounds that all men seek pleasure and avoid pain and that these constitute the fundamental values of all human existence.

In "caring" medicine, the role of the health-care professional is to minimize pain. Of course, pain or discomfort may sometimes be necessary in order to restore health and thus provide further opportunities for pleasure. But the moral judgment is always made by an analysis of probable outcomes. How much pain will be necessary to permit how much quality of life thereafter? The weighing of alternatives as to their anticipated consequences determines the ethically preferred procedure. It is the subsequent quality of life, not the intrinsic sanctity of life, that provides the basis for moral judgment.

The caring model of medical ethics differs from the curing model in that the *consequences* of the action determines its morality, rather than the action itself. Hence, the focus of ethics changes from the issue of right vs. wrong (saving the patient vs. not saving the patient) to that of doing good vs. avoiding harm (saving the patient vs. relieving the patient's suffering). Furthermore, what constitutes care for one person may not be the same as the care desired by another. What one practitioner does to provide care may be different from what another does. The caring approach thus is far more subjective than the curing approach.

The role of the physician changes dramatically in the "caring" approach. Here, the physician becomes a medical consultant, not a healthcare provider. The job is to lay out the options as clearly as possible, explaining to the patient possible procedures, the prognosis for each, probable discomforts and side effects, costs, and risks. Once informed, the patient is responsible for making the choice, and based upon that choice, the physician will proceed, even if that choice does not represent the one the physician would have personally preferred.

Unthinkable Scenarios?

Let me give two examples to illustrate the tension between the curing and caring approaches. The first one is familiar to most of us. Jack Kevorkian has become a household name because of his willingness to assist his terminal patients in committing suicide when their pain becomes too much of a burden and they choose death rather than prolonged suffering. Those who are unable to get the help of Kevorkian can try one of the do-it-yourself techniques described in Derek Humphry's best seller *Final Exit*.

The media have portrayed Kevorkian as a lawbreaker, and at least one reviewer referred to Humphry's book as "ghoulish." But they have forced us into thinking about the unthinkable scenario: I am the one who is terminally ill, facing pain and suffering for the rest of my life, and the cost of prolonging my life is wiping out the money I have saved for my children and grandchildren. What if, on the basis of a utilitarian morality, I conclude that the goal to maximize happiness (for my kin) and minimize pain (for myself) warrants

> *"The sanctity of human life is an important ideal in [the curing] morality."*

my terminating my life? Then the most caring act that a doctor can offer me is to assist me in suicide. Can I turn to my physician or my nurse to help me carry out my decision, or would such help constitute a breach of their medical ethics?

Here is another scenario: Suppose I, a layman in the field of medicine, am the person to whom such an appeal is made by my mother, wife, or daughter. How shall I respond? "The outlook may be dim," I might say, adopting the curing approach, "but one must never give up hope. A remedy might be around the corner; stronger pain relief may be developed; you may go into remission and even recover." Or will my response be based upon the caring approach? Then, understanding my loved one's dilemma and respecting her autonomy, I may begin to explore with her the option of removing vital life-support mechanisms or even assisting in her suicide. In other words, will I do what is right by the law and by traditional morality, or will I do what is good according to a utilitarian or situational morality?

Today we must think about these two "unthinkable" scenarios. At some point in the future, some of us will almost certainly be called upon to render judgment regarding the dilemma. For a lot of people torn between "curing" and "caring," the judgments will not be made easily.

In a film entitled *Code Gray*, which I still use in my medical ethics classes, there is a scene in which an elderly woman in a nursing home is gently confronted by a nurse about a decision to restrain her from leaving the wheelchair and walking about on her own.

"If you fall, you may be seriously injured, and none of us would want that to happen," the nurse explains. But for the elderly woman, her ability to stand up and walk is the last vestige of freedom she enjoys in her old age. To be restrained and forced to call for assistance every time she wants to move about seems too high a price to pay for avoiding the risk of a fall. Nevertheless, the nurse urges her at least to try on the restraint and wear it for a while, and in the end the old woman can do nothing but acquiesce.

In this case, the curing model takes on a new dimension. The woman is not sick or injured, but she risks falling and breaking a bone, becoming disabled. So safety and the preservation of health dictate that she be protected from an accident, even if that means protecting her from herself. On the other hand, while one sympathizes with the old woman, one can also understand why caring for her as she would wish to be cared for would impose an unbearable burden upon the nursing facility. Such facilities are responsible for many elderly persons and are generally not staffed adequately to provide constant surveillance for each patient individually. The use of restraints, tranquilizers, and medications as a way of minimizing risk, therefore, ends up sacrificing caring for safety.

The ethical dilemma we confront here involves the choice between doing what is "right"—e.g., making the woman safe from injury—or doing what results in pleasure—e.g., allowing her the freedom to move about on her own. In choosing to keep the woman safe rather than free, the nursing home opted to do what was "right," even though it resulted in displeasure, rather than to do what was "wrong" (not safeguarding the woman from a fall), even though this would have resulted in the woman's satisfaction.

Tension Between Cure and Care

Many of us who are part of the health-care-delivery system, either as providers or as consumers—and we all eventually are consumers—have been troubled by the tension that is sometimes created between these two approaches. Why do we encounter this tension in contemporary society and how might we learn to deal with it?

"The second approach to medical ethics, 'caring,' is more utilitarian or situational."

The conscientious physician sees death as a defeat, much as good teachers see their students' failure as their own failure. So physicians attempt to conquer injury and disease with whatever technological weapons are available to them, and there is always the possibility of a lawsuit to consider if they waver in seeking a cure. Malpractice insurance is so costly today that it behooves any physician to order every conceivable test and tube and to attach every available monitor in order to escape a legal challenge that begins with the question, "But why didn't you do 'X'?"

To protect themselves from aggressive medical intervention, consumers have also had to resort to legal instruments. The living will, or advance directive, is simply a formalized way to restore to consumers some control over their medical situation. By signing such a document, legal in many states, consumers attempt to prevent aggressive procedures by physicians worried about aggressive lawyers representing aggressive district attorneys, patients, or their next of kin.

> *"The caring model of medical ethics differs from the curing model in that the consequences of the action determines its morality, rather than the action itself."*

Nobody is permitted to trust anybody anymore, it seems, and this means that the health practitioner must always go for the cure, even at the expense of care. Consequently, patients who seek a caring approach had better come to the health-care provider or facility prepared to insist upon their right to decide. This is especially true when the cure may employ complicated medical technology that the patient may not be able to afford.

Patients' express desires are often disregarded. A recent study in the *Journal of the American Medical Association* reported that only about half of the terminally ill patients who had requested do-not-resuscitate orders actually had their wishes respected. Seventy percent of the patients surveyed were never asked their preferences at all.

Of course, not every serious illness creates a confrontation. Physician and patient are often of one mind, so there is no tension. Sometimes, patients are unable or unwilling to assume the responsibilities required of them by the caring model, and they surrender their autonomy to the physician. "You're the doctor. You do what you think best." But occasionally there is no meeting of the minds, and what the physician recommends is not what the patient chooses. Second and third opinions are sought, and patients are left struggling with the consequences of their autonomy at a time when they are least capable of the struggle.

Choices for the Future

The tension between curing and caring in medical ethics is likely to continue, raising some important new issues: What are the duties and rights of patients? What are the roles and responsibilities of providers?

Patients will have to learn enough about their medical condition to make necessary choices. This will not be an easy task because the world of medicine changes so rapidly. If the patient chooses to instruct the providers to do everything possible to attempt a cure, including the use of extraordinary or experimental procedures, does that choice become obligatory upon the providers? Does the patient— any patient—have a right to the best medical services available?

Other questions come to mind. If patient autonomy in medical decisions is to be treated as a right, does this imply a new entitlement to medical services? If the patient cannot finance these services, does the cost of this new entitlement get passed along, in one way or another, to the general public? Does anyone in the medical profession get to veto those procedures deemed too marginal or not cost-effective?

Additional concerns relate directly to physicians. What will become of their role if, for some patients, they attempt every possible procedure for a cure, and for other patients, they act to assist their suicide? Are these two roles professionally and psychologically compatible? Are physicians still professionals under these conditions, or do they become mere paid functionaries for their patients? What happens when their own professional or religious opinions are at odds with the choices of their patients?

In this new world of medicine, the physician will struggle with three alternatives: (1) do what the patient wants, (2) do what common practice requires in order to avoid malpractice suits, or (3) follow his or her own best professional judgment. The second option is the safest choice; the first is realistic only if there is written documentation, as with a living will; and the third is the most risky of all.

Looking for Answers

Ultimately, I as patient will have to place my confidence in my physician. But if I am going to be treated in the manner of my own choosing—either with predisposition toward effecting a cure or toward providing care—I must convey to the physician my attitude regarding a number of very fundamental philosophical questions: How do I view my life at this stage and under these conditions? What do I see as the continuing purpose of my existence? Under what conditions do I wish to exercise my right to maintain my life? Are there conditions in which I would not wish to continue? And what do I want my physician to do for me then?

A living will may answer some of these questions, but I am not so sure that it can convey all of the nuances. And I am not sure my physician will be willing to spend the time it takes to listen, especially if that physician is not my primary care provider, but someone to whom I have been referred and whom I do not know. Most significantly, when the time comes, I am not at all sure I will have the answers to those questions. I don't have them now, and I'm not optimistic that somehow they will be revealed to me in my hour of need.

"The living will, or advance directive, is simply a formalized way to restore to consumers some control over their medical situation."

Despite the pile of literature that keeps growing on this subject, medical ethics is troubled today, but it is not the fault of medical ethicists, or even of lawyers, physicians, hospitals, or nursing homes. And it is not the fault of patients. It is merely a reflection of the fact that we are all troubled today by the complexity of technology, by the innumerable options and choices, and by the larger questions about the purpose of being alive. Now, more than ever, we need the wisdom of a Socrates to remind us that, of all our obligations, the primary one is to "know thyself." Attaining that would go a long way toward resolving these dilemmas.

Physicians Should Not Provide Futile Treatment

by Nancy S. Jecker and Lawrence J. Schneiderman

About the authors: Nancy S. Jecker is a professor in the department of medical history and ethics at the University of Washington School of Medicine in Seattle. Lawrence J. Schneiderman is a professor of community and family medicine at the University of California School of Medicine in San Diego.

Physicians and other health professionals sometimes find themselves continuing aggressive medical procedures well beyond the point at which such measures would be useful. The impetus for this may come from a variety of sources. Perhaps the patient, fearful of death, desperately seeks every conceivable way to avoid it. Alternatively, a family member or loved one may implore the health care team to "do everything possible" and "spare no expense" when a patient is unconscious or delirious and unable to speak for himself or herself.

Nonbeneficial Medical Treatments

Sometimes it is physicians or other members of the health care team who insist on nonbeneficial medical treatments because they cannot let go. The reasons for this may lie in the emotional bonding that takes place between a desperately ill patient and dedicated providers, or may lie in misguided notions of ethical or legal obligation. Perhaps a physician has already "saved" the patient from the brink of death on several occasions, and feels that giving up now would mean that these previous efforts were of no avail. Or perhaps members of the health care team regard death as a personal failure, to be avoided at all costs. Perhaps, too, education and training has inculcated in health providers a bias toward action; therefore, standing by and "doing nothing" in the face of death seems inconceivable. Finally, in this day when the practice of medicine has been opened up to public scrutiny and ethical dilemmas sometimes become media spectacles, pressure to continue extreme life-prolonging treatments may come from outsiders with political, religious, or other motives. These and other attitudes give rise to situations in which medical interventions are used despite overwhelming evidence that they will not benefit the patient.

One example of nonbeneficial medical treatment is mechanical ventilation (the respirator) employed on a patient in a permanent vegetative state, a condition characterized by permanent unconsciousness. Because the patient is utterly incapable of appreciation, and will never appreciate, ventilator assistance as a benefit, the treatment strikes us as unambiguously futile. Almost as clearly futile, in our opinion, is attempting cardiopulmonary resuscitation on a terminally ill cancer patient whose death is imminent

> *"Not only are health professionals not obligated to provide nonbeneficial treatments, they are obligated not to provide such treatments."*

and who is experiencing unremitting pain and discomfort or is under heavy sedation. In this case, the harms of the procedure (more misery from invasive intubation, broken ribs, organ damage including possible brain damage) must be weighed against the potential benefits (a few more hours or days in the intensive care unit). Another example of futile treatment is tube-feeding a patient with multiple organ failure whose condition is so irreversible that the patient will never leave the intensive care unit of a hospital.

In all of these instances, although the intervention produces an *effect* on the patient's body, it fails to provide a *benefit* to the patient as a whole. If the goal of health care is to heal (from Old English "to make whole") the patient (from the Latin for "suffer"), then such interventions are inappropriate—or futile. We argue that not only are health professionals not obligated to provide nonbeneficial treatments, they are obligated *not* to provide such treatments, because they violate ethical standards of the health care professions. The purpose of this viewpoint is: (a) to clarify the meaning of medical futility; (b) to illustrate, through actual case examples, the application of medical futility; and (c) to urge increased efforts to provide more appropriate, care-oriented treatments when life-sustaining measures are futile.

When Is an Intervention Futile?

We define a medical treatment as "futile" in situations where either the *likelihood* of benefiting the patient is so vanishingly small as to be unrealistic or the *quality* of benefit to be gained is so minimal that the health goals of medicine are not being achieved. We refer to these two situations as quantitative and qualitative futility, respectively.

Informed and well-intentioned people may disagree about the specific levels at which quantitative and qualitative definitions of medical futility can be drawn. For example, people may set different cut-off points regarding how low the odds of success must be for a treatment to be futile. This is not surprising because where one sets the cut-off point for quantitative futility involves a value judgment. What counts as an acceptable chance? Likewise there may not be unanimous agreement about what qualities of outcomes are poor enough to qualify as futile. Again, the judgment of futility requires a value decision.

Some may prefer to wait for "absolute certainty" before making judgments about futility. As pointed out by philosophers as venerable as John Stuart Mill and as contemporary as Karl Popper, however, absolute certainty is an absolute impossibility. We can never be certain about the presence of causal connections in life, much less in medicine. We can draw conclusions only in a common-sense way after making empirical observations. In formulating a specific approach to medical futility, therefore, one should look for a common-sense account. We propose calling an intervention quantitatively futile if experience has shown that it has less than 1 chance in 100 of benefiting the patient. With respect to qualitative futility, we identify several exemplar cases. The most obvious we have already cited: the patient in permanent vegetative state—of whom it is estimated that perhaps as many as 35,000 in the USA alone are being kept alive by artificial nutrition and hydration. There can be no treatment of any benefit to such a patient. Another situation is the patient whose illness confines him or her permanently to the intensive care unit, where the magnitude of benefit is dubious because treatment requires the patient's entire preoccupation to the exclusion of other life goals.

Prolonging Life Does Not Always Benefit Patients

One problem with applying this definition in practice is that health providers and family members sometimes interpret the patient's plea to "Do everything!" to mean doing everything possible to prolong life—even at great cost in suffering and dignity. An interpretation more consonant with the ethical traditions of health care however, is that it is incumbent on physicians and other health professionals to do everything possible to benefit patients, including maximizing comfort and dignity when life prolongation is neither reasonable nor desired. The idea that health providers are obligated to prolong biological life for its own sake is a modern idea, an idea without precedent in health care's ethical traditions. Hippocratic physicians, for example, shunned the use of futile treatments in order to distinguish themselves from charlatans. Hippocratic physicians were expected to recognize when a disease "overmastered" known medical treatments and to refrain from using such treatments. The emphasis of Hippocratic medicine was to restore the patient's health where possible, and to alleviate the patient's suffering. Sadly, in modern times, health care teams sometimes become preoccupied with life-prolongation efforts and overlook the duty to care for patients. It is important to emphasize that although *treatment* may be futile, *caring* for patients and patients' loved ones never is.

> *"We propose calling an intervention quantitatively futile if experience has shown that it has less than 1 chance in 100 of benefiting the patient."*

Chapter 1

Physicians Are Not Obligated to Provide Futile Treatment

When a patient or family member insists on continuing futile treatments, the health care team has no obligation to provide such treatments. After all, as we have said, the goal of health care is to benefit the patient. When treatment ceases to provide a benefit, there is no clear reason to continue with it. Furthermore, providing futile treatments often violates the health care provider's duty

> *"The idea that health providers are obligated to prolong biological life for its own sake is a modern idea, an idea without precedent in health care's ethical traditions."*

not to harm patients because such treatments are often invasive and burdensome, only adding pointlessly to the patient's pain and discomfort. Finally, the use of futile treatments should be avoided because it wastes society's resources. Typically, interventions that are futile are also costly, requiring the use of expensive

medical technologies, the attention of multiple health care providers, and the use of hospital beds that other patients may need.

Some have argued that patients have a right to be autonomous or self-determining agents and that denying futile treatments to patients deprives them of this right. Yet, in response, it can be said that although autonomy guarantees a competent adult patient the right to refuse any medical treatment, it does not guarantee the patient a right to obtain any medical treatment. Whereas the former, negative right, simply asks others not to interfere, the latter, positive right, requires actions on the part of others who also have a right to be autonomous and self-determining. Patients cannot ethically compel physicians, nurses, and other health care workers to provide treatment that violates the health care provider's own conscientiously held personal beliefs, or the standards of the health profession to which the individual belongs. No other profession labors under an unlimited mandate of the people it serves. A lawyer, for example, is obligated to provide a vigorous and competent defense for a client accused of murder. But a lawyer is not obligated to do *anything* the client wants—phone the governor, phone the President—since the lawyer is responsible also to the reasonable standards of the legal profession.

Baby K

To illustrate medical futility's meaning and ethical implications, we now describe two real cases involving the use of futile interventions. The first was reported in the popular press and concerns an intervention, cardiopulmonary resuscitation, that in this case was qualitatively futile because the patient will never be conscious or appreciate any benefit from treatment. Thus, treatment serves merely to prolong biological life, without benefiting the patient as a person.

Baby K was born with a condition known as anencephaly, in which most of the brain—except for rudimentary portions of the lower brain—are missing. The doctors caring for Baby K know that Baby K will never think, hear, see or indeed perform any of the activities that we associate with a living person, except for so-called "vegetative functions," such as breathing (with the help of a machine), digestion, and urine formation. Now 16 months old, Baby K is placed on a mechanical ventilator whenever Baby K has trouble breathing, following the patient's mother's wishes. Although the patient lives at a nursing home, the patient has been taken to a hospital in Fairfax, Virginia, at least three times with severe respiratory problems.

The child's mother has insisted that doctors "do everything" for Baby K, and has stated that she wants God, not the health care team, to decide when her child will die. Yet Baby K's doctors have argued that mechanical ventilation will do nothing to replace absent brain tissue and therefore ameliorate the child's underlying condition. The hospital where Baby K is being treated requested court permission to deny emergency treatment.

The child has spent about 120 days at the Fairfax Hospital, at a minimum cost of $174,000, paid for by State Medicaid and private insurance.

In response to this case, some may argue that biological life itself is sacred or has intrinsic value, and therefore Baby K's life should be continued. Yet even if this position is correct, again we emphasize the ends of medicine (and other health professionals) are not to keep bodies alive but to benefit patients. Doctors' and nurses' commitment is to persons, not to biological life as such. Nor do medicine and nursing function simply as instruments to carry out others' (family's or patient's) wishes. Rather, as professions, medicine and nursing uphold certain standards and values as their own. Continuing to provide futile treatment to Baby K undermines the integrity and goals of the health care team. Furthermore, futile treatment for Baby K expends society's finite resources, and may violate principles of justice in the allocation of society's resources.

> *"Although **treatment** may be futile, **caring** for patients and patients' loved ones never is."*

A Hopelessly Ill AIDS Patient

In contrast to case 1, consider the following case involving a young man in the terminal stages of acquired immunodeficiency syndrome (AIDS). One of us (L.J.S.) was involved in an ethics consultation involving this patient. Members of the health care team were attempting to decide whether or not to recommend terminating life support measures for the patient, and shifting the emphasis of treatment to palliative and comfort measures.

A 36-year old male bartender is admitted for the third time to the intensive care unit with complications from AIDS, including Kaposi's sarcoma (a form of cancer), pneumocystic pneumonia, idiopathic thrombocytopenia purpura (a severe blood clotting disorder) and disseminated mycobacterium intracellulare avium (a tuberculosis-like infection). Over the several days in the intensive care unit he developed failure in several organ systems, including the lungs, kidneys, liver, heart, and became progressively obtunded (out-of-it). Although the man's partner at first insisted that "everything be done" to keep him alive, it soon became apparent to the physicians involved in the case that, from previous experience with patients in this condition, the patient had no realistic chance of survival.

Recognizing the futility of life support efforts, the physicians requested an ethics consultation. The outcome of discussion among members of the health care team was a decision that treatment objectives should be changed from "full code (do resuscitate), full care" to "no code (do not resuscitate), comfort care."

Members of the health care team did their best to persuade the patient's partner to accept the patient's impending death and assist with efforts to contact family members and friends. After extended discussions, the patient's partner agreed. The health care team used a morphine drip to keep the patient comfortable, and pillows to prop up the patient to make his breathing easier. The patient's partner, family members, and friends, recognizing that death was imminent, visited the patient and said their farewells. The patient died a few days later.

"The use of futile treatments should be avoided because it wastes society's resources."

In sharp contrast to case 1, case 2 reached a point of moral and emotional closure for the health care team and for those who were close to the patient. Rather than using futile treatments as perhaps a symbolic show of love and concern, more fitting measures were used to convey caring. Although death is always an occasion for grief and sadness, in this instance medicine did not fail to offer solace in the face of it.

Accepting Death

The foregoing discussion suggests what doctors and nurses should be doing when they can no longer cure or ameliorate disease because death is imminent: they should offer comfort to patients and loved ones. Rather than abandoning the patient or those who are close to the patient, health care providers should instead assure their continued support, and should use low technology, care-oriented measures that offer relief and dignity to the patient. Simple acts, such as holding a patient's hand, moistening a patient's lips, talking and listening to a patient and loved ones, are very much a part of health care as are the latest high technology machines and gadgets. Sadly, modern health care has sometimes lost sight of this, and providers have sometimes neglected their obligation to help patients and families in these ways.

Rather than viewing the end of life as a medical failure, we submit that health professionals should instead regard death as a planned-for and natural event. Rather than understanding the impending loss of a loved one as an occasion to defy death, we have argued that family and friends should instead help patients and each other to face death with courage and dignity.

Physician-Assisted Suicide Is Consistent with Medical Ethics

by Timothy E. Quill, Lonny J. Shavelson, and Fred S. Marcus

About the authors: *Timothy E. Quill is a hospice physician and the author of* Death with Dignity: Making Choices and Taking Charge. *Lonny J. Shavelson is a physician and the author of* A Chosen Death: The Dying Confront Assisted Suicide. *Fred S. Marcus is a physician and president of the Death with Dignity National Center.*

> "I am a retired general surgeon . . . dependent on a respirator. . . . When my continued survival is no longer meaningful (to me), I hope that a caring physician will make the transition as easy as possible. . . . I realize that some health professionals will find it impossible to do this, but I hope they and society will understand the true compassion for their patients' suffering that motivates the physicians who do help those in need."
>
> —Stewart A. King, M.D.

In taking the Hippocratic Oath, doctors promise to prolong their patients' lives and to minimize human suffering. When these two simple directives seemingly conflict, as they do when a terminally-ill patient experiences irreversible, intolerable suffering prior to his or her death, the physician enters an uncharted territory.

But what responsibility or obligation does a physician bear when death is the only way to end suffering and when continued life can only promise further disintegration and relentless suffering? We believe that this situation constitutes a medical emergency; it requires a creative, compassionate response that fully respects the values of the patient, the patient's family, and the physician.

Relieving Suffering

The medical profession generally agrees that a physician's central mission in caring for the dying should be to use both personal and medical resources to relieve the symptoms and to maintain the patient's integrity.

Reprinted from Timothy E. Quill, Lonny J. Shavelson, and Fred S. Marcus, "The Issue: From the Physicians' Perspective," web article at www.deathwithdignity.org/informed/perspectives/physpers1.html, by permission of the authors and the Death with Dignity National Center. Revised and updated by the authors.

Clinicians, ethicists, and lawyers also agree that this includes measures that may indirectly contribute to death, such as high-dose medicines or withdrawal of life supports. Many feel as we do that the difference between removing life supports and providing the means for a chosen death is an artificial distinction, that is, there is no major ethical difference between these two acts. However, medicine has not reached consensus on this point.

We believe that hospice care is the standard of care for the dying, and physician-assisted dying should be the measure of last resort. It should be used rarely, when all other alternatives have been fully explored and found to be ineffective or unacceptable. But when a competent patient requests such assistance, direct aid in dying is one of the most profound and meaningful acts that a physician can perform. Moreover, on rare occasions, it is sometimes the only way to prevent the abandonment of those most in need, those whose suffering is most extreme.

As caregivers, each of us draws moral lines around our responsibilities. But when a dying patient is rapidly deteriorating and requests our help in achieving a peaceful, dignified death, it is sometimes necessary for us to re-consider those boundaries. Whether we assist or whether we hold back because of religious, social, legal, or personal values, the choice we make has a profound and lasting effect on both the sufferer and the caregiver.

The patient and family may have no choices. We *do*. We believe that as caring physicians, we need to challenge our own preconceptions and to sometimes set them aside to make sure real choices exist for our patients.

Clinical Criteria for Physician-Assisted Death

Drawing on the criteria originally proposed in several scholarly journals physicians, ethicists, and legal authorities within the right-to-die movement have suggested that the following clinical criteria be applied to the process of considering a request for physician-assisted dying:

- The patient clearly and repeatedly of his or her own free will requests to die rather than to continue suffering.
- The patient's judgment is not distorted.
- The patient's condition is incurable. It is associated with severe, unrelenting, intolerable suffering, and all reasonable means of relief have been fully explored.
- The physician ensures that the patient's suffering and the request are not due to inadequate comfort care.
- Physician-assisted death is carried out only within the context of a meaningful doctor-patient relationship.
- Consultation with another independent physician who is skilled in palliative care is required.
- Clear documentation supporting each of the above conditions is required.

Physicians Should Be Permitted to Assist in Suicide

by Marcia Angell

About the author: *Marcia Angell is executive editor of the* New England Journal of Medicine.

Editor's note: The following viewpoint was written in response to the Supreme Court's 1997 decisions in Washington v. Glucksberg *and* Vacco v. Quill, *in which the Court ruled that terminally ill patients do not have a constitutionally protected right to physician-assisted suicide.*

No one trusts the dying to know what they want. The U.S. Supreme Court found dying patient have no right to decide for themselves to cut short their suffering by asking their doctors to prescribe an overdose of sleeping pills or painkillers. According to the court, it is not a decision for patients and doctors, but for state legislatures, most of which have laws on the books prohibiting doctor-assisted suicide. Unless states change their laws, dying patients are to march on like good soldiers, denied this most desperate of choices.

The Supreme Court missed the point: Dying can be slow and agonizing, and some people simply want to get it over with. Good palliative care usually can help, but not always and often not enough. The problem is not just pain, although that can be devastating. Other symptoms, such as breathlessness and nausea, can be worse and even harder to relieve.

And there are no good treatments for weakness, immobility and helplessness—probably the most important reasons for despair in those dying slowly, along with the knowledge that the condition is irreversible.

Fortunately, not every dying person faces such suffering, but some do, despite the best efforts of their doctors. What option do they have? If they are on some

Reprinted from Marcia Angell, "No One Trusts the Dying," *The Washington Post*, July 7, 1997, by permission of the author.

life support like a ventilator, they legally can have it turned off. But often they aren't on life support.

A Personal Choice

I see no reason for the state to require such patients to die slowly, regardless of their wishes. After all, we are not talking about life vs. death, but about the manner of dying. Nor are we talking about "killing," despite some of the over-heated rhetoric. We are talking about choice—the same sort of choice the Supreme Court honors in a host of other personal decisions, such as abortion, marriage and sexual behavior. Dying patients suffering intractably should have the option of taking an overdose, just as they now have the option of turning off life supports. Probably in most cases, they never would take the pills, but they would have the peace of mind of knowing they had a choice.

Doctors, for their part, would also have a choice. They would not have to comply with requests for an overdose, any more than they are required to per-form abortions, but they would have the option of doing so without becoming criminals. As for the argument that dying patients would be "pressured" to ask for assisted suicide, there is no evidence that they or their families are now "pressured" to refuse life supports, even though that is at least as likely.

The Supreme Court clearly had a hard time with this decision. Even though the vote was 9–0 against doctor-assisted suicide, the justices

"Compassionate doctors always have helped patients to end their lives."

wrote several different opinions. Underlying them all, though, was the notion that permitting doctor-assisted suicide would be too great a departure from tra-dition, and besides, good palliative care should relieve all suffering. The court was wrong on both counts.

Physician-Assisted Death in the Real World

Compassionate doctors always have helped dying patients to end their lives. They do so not only by turning off life supports, but by giving large doses of morphine or by prescribing more sleeping pills than necessary. The problem is that the practice is secret and unpredictable, depending more on doctors' courage and compassion than on patients' needs and wishes. As for good pallia-tive care, I defer to no one in my belief in its importance, but it is not an alter-native to doctor-assisted suicide, which should be used only when palliative care fails.

The court also accepted distinctions that have little meaning in the real world, although they are important to many lawyers and some doctors and ethicists. It held that turning off life supports is acceptable because it is merely the rejection of unwanted treatment, whereas suicide is not because it actively causes death. And it held that giving an overdose of morphine is acceptable when it is prescribed to relieve pain, not to cause death.

In reality, when a dying patient's life supports are turned off, it is seldom because the treatment itself is burdensome, but mainly because the patient or the family wants to hasten death. And when doctors give high doses of morphine at the end of a dying patient's life, they often want to bring about a quicker as well as a more comfortable death. The public is not caught up with these legalistic distinctions, probably because so many people have seen loved ones die unnecessarily hard and prolonged deaths. Polls consistently show that about two-thirds of the public favor permitting doctor-assisted suicide.

An Unjust Decision

I wish the Supreme Court had recognized a constitutional right to doctor-assisted suicide for dying patients. It is the most personal and private matter, and it should be decided that way, not as a political matter in state legislatures. But sooner or later, one way or another, the practice will become legal, because dying patients need that choice, and their doctors need to be able to help them. For the state to require dying patients to endure unrelievable suffering is callous and unseemly. Death is hard enough without being bullied.

Physicians Should Not Withhold Lifesaving Treatments

by Wesley J. Smith

About the author: *Wesley J. Smith is an attorney for the International Anti-Euthanasia Task Force and the author of* Forced Exit: The Slippery Slope from Assisted Suicide to Legalized Murder.

Former news anchorman Hugh Finn was intentionally dehydrated to death in November 1998, when doctors at a Manassas, Virginia, nursing home removed his feeding tube at the request of his wife, Michele. The act was legal. It had the explicit approval of federal and Virginia courts. It took eight days for Finn to die.

Finn was not terminally ill. He was left severely brain damaged by a 1995 automobile accident. His doctors claimed he would always remain unconscious, in what is known as a permanent vegetative state. But there was significant reason for doubt. His brother Ed claimed that Hugh was sometimes conscious and interactive, as did other members of the Finn family. A medical investigator testified that Hugh Finn had said "Hi" to her upon their first meeting, which if true proved Finn was conscious. The judge in the case refused to allow time for further investigation. Now Finn is dead, and we will never know the truth.

Hastening Death Has Become Routine

Finn's death made headlines because of the intervention of Virginia governor James Gilmore on the side of Finn's brothers and parents, who wanted feeding to continue. And many people around the country expressed shock at his fate. They shouldn't have. For years, the medical intelligentsia—philosophers, academics, and policy advocates known as bioethicists—have pushed lawmakers and judges to permit the death of patients like Hugh Finn who depend on feeding tubes for nutrition and water. In 1990, the Supreme Court gave its implied permission to the practice in the Nancy Cruzan case. Today, people diagnosed as being in a permanent vegetative state are deprived of food and water almost as a matter of medical routine. Moreover, *conscious* brain-damaged patients meet the same end. Indeed, families of profoundly brain-damaged people are often pressured by doctors and social workers to cease "treatment" with food and fluids as a way of easing family burdens and ending lives deemed to have poor quality.

> *"In futile-care cases, it isn't the treatment that theorists see as futile, but the patients."*

It is only when families are divided, as they were in the Finn case, that such cases end up in court. But if the patient is in a vegetative state, it is almost impossible to stop a dehydration ordered by a spouse or other primary medical decision-maker, no matter how strongly other members of the family may object. If the patient is conscious, it remains a harder sell to obtain court permission for dehydration and starvation over family objections. But it is doubtful that the courts will resist for much longer.

Alarming Cases

Take the 1995 Michael Martin case in Michigan. Mary Martin wanted to dehydrate her husband, who was brain-damaged from an auto accident. She was opposed in court by Michael's mother and sister, who presented medical testimony that he was conscious, enjoyed television and music, and had indicated a desire to live. (He could communicate with head nods and shakes.) Notwithstanding this testimony, and despite the wife's admission that she would benefit financially from her husband's death, the trial court and the Michigan Court of Appeals ordered the dehydration to proceed. Michael is alive today only because the Michigan Supreme Court ruled that Mary had failed to demonstrate by clear and convincing evidence that Michael, in his current condition, would want to die. Had she been able to do so, the dehydration would have occurred.

A strikingly similar case involving a Stockton, California, man named Robert Wendland is now playing out in the courts. Robert was severely injured in a 1993 auto accident. He was unconscious for about 16 months—during which time California law would have explicitly permitted his dehydration. Then, he awakened and learned to maneuver his wheelchair down a hospital corridor and perform other simple tasks on request. Still, his wife Rose wants him dehydrated to death, contending that he would not want to live in a dependent condition. Robert Wendland would be dead today but for an anonymous whistleblower who alerted Robert's mother, Florence Wendland, and his sister, Rebekah Vinson. They sued to keep Robert alive.

The litigation has been bitter and prolonged. Robert's interests were supposed to be represented by a San Joaquin County public defender, Doran Berg. But in a nasty twist, Berg sided with the wife and argued even more vehemently and emotionally *for* Robert's dehydration than Rose did—perhaps the first time in the history of jurisprudence that a public defender has urged a judge to sentence a client to death. But Judge Bob McNatt reluctantly declined. Stating that he was making "the absolutely wrong decision, for all the right reasons," McNatt ruled wisely that such a momentous change in law and ethics should be decided in the legislature or a court of appeals, not by a trial judge.

McNatt's December 9, 1997 decision may have been only a reprieve for Robert Wendland. Berg quickly appealed and asked McNatt to authorize the use of San Joaquin County funds for a private attorney to argue for Robert's death in the appeals courts. McNatt agreed and permitted a maximum fee of $50,000. The power of the state of California and the money of its taxpayers are now being used to urge the death of one of its citizens, whose only "crime" is to be brain-damaged.

"Futile-Care Theory"

Cases such as Hugh Finn's, Michael Martin's, and Robert Wendland's are usually described in the media as promoting patient autonomy and private medical decision-making by families. But that is only partly true. Increasingly, "choice" in medical cases involving the profoundly disabled people is viewed by bioethicists and doctors as a one-way street. Should families choose death for their loved ones, their wishes are honored and acted on with dispatch. But if families insist that their brain-damaged loved ones continue to be nourished and cared for, these same experts proclaim instead that "autonomy has its limits."

> *"Doctors and hospitals . . . have already refused to provide desired medical treatment to profoundly disabled and dying patients."*

This doctrine, little known among the general public but all the rage in bioethics, is called "futile-care theory." The theory goes like this: When a patient reaches a certain predefined stage of age, illness, or disability, any further care other than pain-relief is "futile" and should be withheld, regardless of the desires of the patient or family. The name is a bit duplicitous. In futile-care cases, it isn't the treatment that theorists see as futile, but the patients. Treatment isn't supposed to be stopped because it has no effect, but because it does.

Already Widespread

Futile-care decisions are already being implemented in many of the nation's hospitals. Little noticed by the mainstream media—but well documented in the medical literature—doctors and hospitals in Michigan, Massachusetts, Texas, Tennessee, and California have already refused to provide desired medical treatment to profoundly disabled and dying patients. This has led to a handful of court cases. In 1993, when doctors at Hurley Medical Center in Flint, Michigan, decided to remove life support from Baby Terry, a prematurely born infant with little chance of survival, his parents objected. Terry had gained a pound and successfully fought off a bacterial infection since his birth, and his parents hoped for a miracle. Their decision landed them in court, where a judge—*solely* on the basis of their refusal to terminate life support—stripped them of their right as parents to make medical decisions for their son. Baby Terry died as the case was being appealed.

The parents of Baby Ryan, in Spokane, Washington, had a similar experience the following year. Ryan was born after only 23 weeks of gestation and required kidney dialysis to remain alive. After determining that he was not a suitable candidate for organ donation, his doctors declared that any further treatment of Ryan was futile, and they removed him from dialysis over the explicit objection of his parents. Ryan would have died, but his parents sued and obtained a temporary court order to continue treatment. Eventually, Ryan was transferred to Legacy Emanuel Children's Hospital in Portland, Oregon, where he was soon weaned off dialysis. Had Ryan's original doctors successfully imposed their futile-care philosophy, Ryan would be dead today instead of a living 4-year-old boy.

A current lawsuit over futile care involves Mercy Medical Center, of Redding, California, and Dr. Lang Dayton, a local physician. In 1996, Beverly Williamson was admitted to Mercy with septic shock and renal failure caused by a previously undiagnosed cancer. Doctors couldn't figure out what was wrong and spent nearly two months treating her and conducting extensive medical tests, which finally revealed that Beverly had terminal-stage cancer.

Beverly would undoubtedly die. So, Dr. Dayton wrote a letter to her family telling them of his intention to cease further life-supporting treatment based on his determination that it was "futile" because it would "prolong her suffering and not save her life." Beverly's family objected immediately and in writing, in deference to Beverly's oft-stated, deeply held desires about the level of care she wanted at the end of her life. But the hospital's ethics committee overrode the family's objections and gave Dr. Dayton permission to cut off Beverly's treatment. Six days later, her life support was removed and she died later that day. The family sued. The case is expected to go to trial [in 1999].

> *"Had Ryan's original doctors successfully imposed their futile-care philosophy, Ryan would be dead today instead of a living 4-year-old boy."*

Futile-care theory is so new that the state of the law has not kept pace with clinical practice, leaving families, lawyers, and clinicians in doubt as to their respective rights and obligations. But many medical associations have now endorsed the doctrine, which means that desperately ill and disabled patients will increasingly be denied treatment against their families' and their wishes. Lawsuits are sure to follow.

To better defend themselves in court, many hospitals have begun quietly to adopt formal futile-care policies that they hope judges will enforce. Typical of such policies is the one instituted last year by the Alexian Brothers Hospital in San Jose, California. The Alexian Brothers "Non-Beneficial Care Policy" creates a presumption that requests for medical treatment (including such low-tech

> *"[Futile-care policies] are also underpinned, let's face it, by a cold-hearted, collectivist desire to save 'scarce resources' by throwing society's weakest members out of the lifeboat."*

interventions as antibiotics, tube feeding, and medical testing, as well as high-tech treatments such as dialysis) are "inappropriate" for patients with severe illnesses or profound disabilities, such as permanent vegetative state, permanent dependence on intensive care, and terminal illnesses in the final stage. The only care such patients are generally supposed to receive at Alexian Brothers is comfort care—regardless of their families' or their desires.

Doctors who wish to provide "inappropriate" treatment must "provide written justification." Hospital personnel are urged to report doctors who violate the guidelines to the medical director. The punishment for deviation from the policy is unmentioned, but the one club every hospital holds over doctors is the suspension or withdrawal of staff privileges. Patients and families who disagree with the hospital's determination of futility must find another hospital. And if no other hospital will take the patient? The policy is silent.

In New York, legislation has been introduced to clarify the rights and obligations of decision-makers and health-care providers when a patient is incompetent. Alarmingly, if passed in their current form, the bills would set futile-care theory into legal concrete. The measures would permit hospitals to refuse desired treatment if based on a "formally adopted policy" predicated on "sincerely held moral convictions." Physicians, too, could refuse to treat patients if doing so violated their moral beliefs. Disputes about treatment would be taken to committees that the legislation would require each hospital to create. If the person speaking for the patient disagreed with the decision of the ethics committee, he would have to move his loved one to a different hospital. Doctors and hospitals that acted in "good faith" pursuant to the law would be granted immunity to civil and criminal penalties. Opponents of the measures are hoping to require that care of the patient continue until a doctor can be found willing to provide the desired treatment.

Rule by the Strong

Futile-care policies are ostensibly designed to relieve the suffering of desperately ill and disabled people. But they are also underpinned, let's face it, by a cold-hearted, collectivist desire to save "scarce resources" by throwing society's weakest members out of the lifeboat. Futile-care theorists would refuse desired end-of-life treatment to Grandma Jones in Florida so that Little Suzie in

40

Appalachia could have better access to medical care. Among bioethics professionals, for whom such a restructuring of society is a deeply treasured goal, this is known as "distributive justice."

But let's give the movement its proper name: rule by the strong. People on the medical margins are the first victims of the distributive-justice movement because they are widely viewed as having lives of little meaning or purpose. They can't or don't protest. And with remarkably few exceptions, no one else protests their fate either. As a result, futile-care theorists encounter surprisingly little opposition as they carve into the bedrock of American law the utilitarian principle that the lives of some people can be sacrificed for the benefit of others deemed more worthy of care.

Futile-care policies, in and of themselves, won't save that much money. But once futile-care theory is legally entrenched, America's traditional medical system—organized around preserving the life and health of the individual patient and the Hippocratic obligation of the doctor to care

> *"Let's give the movement its proper name: rule by the strong."*

for that patient—will be enfeebled beyond recognition. We will then be well down the path to wholesale health-care rationing—a topic that is already of consuming interest to bioethicists. Seen in this light, the food and fluid cases and the coming futile-care disputes do not represent the end of a legal debate over individual choice and patient autonomy. They are in fact the beginning of a larger struggle for control of health-care decision-making by an elite caste of hospital administrators, doctors, and bioethicists who share an unwholesome interest in arbitrating who is worthy—and who is unworthy—of keeping alive.

Physician-Assisted Suicide Violates Medical Ethics

by Daniel Callahan

About the author: Daniel Callahan is cofounder and president of the Hastings Center and author of numerous books on medical ethics, including The Troubled Dream of Life: In Search of a Peaceful Death.

[An] argument one often hears both in the Netherlands and in this country is that euthanasia and assisted suicide are perfectly compatible with the aims of medicine. I would note at the very outset that a physician who participates in another person's suicide already abuses medicine. Apart from depression (the main statistical cause of suicide), people commit suicide because they find life empty, oppressive, or meaningless. Their judgment is a judgment about the value of continued life, not only about health (even if they are sick). Are doctors now to be given the right to make judgments about the kinds of life worth living and to give their blessing to suicide for those they judge wanting? What conceivable competence, technical or moral, could doctors claim to play such a role? Are we to medicalize suicide, turning judgments about its worth and value into one more clinical issue?

The Limits of Medicine

Yes, those are rhetorical questions, yet they bring us to the core of the problem of euthanasia, physician-assisted suicide (PAS), and medicine. The great temptation of modern medicine, not always resisted, is to move beyond the promotion and preservation of health into the boundless realm of general human happiness and well-being. The root problem of illness and mortality is both medical and philosophical or religious. Why must I die? can be asked as a technical, biological question or as a question about the meaning of life. When medicine tries to respond to the latter, which it is always under pressure to do, it moves beyond its proper role. Medicine has no special insight into the meaning of life or the meaning of a life marked by suffering and death.

It is not medicine's place to lift from us the burden of that suffering which turns on the meaning we assign to the decay of the body and its eventual death. It is not medicine's place to determine when lives are not worth living or when the burden of life is too great to be borne. Doctors have no conceivable way of evaluating such claims on the part of patients, and they should have no right to act in response to them. Medicine should try to relieve human suffering, but only that suffering which is brought on by illness and dying as biological phenomena, not that suffering which comes from anguish or despair at the human condition.

Doctors Must Comfort, but Never Kill

Doctors ought to relieve those forms of suffering that medically accompany serious illness and the threat of death. They should relieve pain, do what they can to allay anxiety and uncertainty, and be a comforting presence. As sensitive human beings, doctors should be prepared to respond to patients who ask why they must die or die in pain. But here the doctor and the patient are at the same level. The doctor may have no better answer to those old questions than anyone else and certainly no special insight from his training as a physician. It would be terrible for physicians to forget this and to think that in a swift, lethal injection or in the provision of suicide pills, medicine has found its own technical answer to the riddle of life.

Physicians ought not to abandon their critically ill, suffering patients. They should accompany them to the

> *"It is not medicine's place to determine when lives are not worth living."*

end. But it is not abandonment for a physician to refuse to step over that line which separates the medical struggle against pain, suffering, and death from the active pursuit of death, to positively seek death as the answer to the problem of life. That is to fundamentally compromise the nature of medicine, to mistake its skill with the lethal tools of death as a warrant for the bringing of death to relieve a patient of the burden of life. But would this be true even in those cases where it was the earlier actions of the physician that perhaps brought on the pain and suffering of a critical or terminal illness? Do not physicians have a duty to relieve that suffering which was caused by their treatment?

Suffering and Death Are Inevitable

This seems a false conclusion. If patients understand that doctors do not have a moral license to commit euthanasia or engage in PAS and also give their informed consent to treatment, they can hardly blame the physician if, despite good intentions, the treatment does not turn out well. Nor does it follow that because a doctor was a causal source of pain and suffering, doctors should be able to directly kill patients or help them kill themselves by way of reparation. Medicine is an uncertain art and a less than perfect science. There is no call for reparation when it fails, nor is unavoidable pain and suffering to be understood as a failure of medicine. Human bodies must fail and eventually die. It can hardly be made an obligation on the part of medicine to be held responsible for that biological state of affairs. Nor can it be a right of patients to claim that doctors must set the world right when it goes wrong.

The Corruption of Medicine

A final word. It is not within the power of medicine—and probably never will be—to master life and death and to control nature. It *ought* never to be within the moral power of medicine to use its skills to bring about death, whether directly or indirectly. A medicine that took on that role would soon corrupt itself, inevitably falling into abuse and assuming a kind of power it ought not to have; and it would inevitably corrupt the rest of us as well, turning to medicine to relieve us of the weight and meaning of life. Medicine does not and cannot have that kind of wisdom, and it surely would not gain it by acting as our agent in death.

Physicians Should Not Be Permitted to Assist in Suicide

by Rita L. Marker

About the author: *Rita L. Marker is an attorney and executive director of the International Anti-Euthanasia Task Force.*

Of all public controversies in recent years, assisted suicide perhaps is the one surrounded by the greatest degree of misunderstanding. For example, one often hears it referred to as the "right to die." Yet assisted suicide has nothing to do with letting someone die. Neither the law nor medical ethics requires that a person be kept alive by being subjected to unwanted medical treatment.

Furthermore, the debate isn't about the tragic, personal act of suicide, nor is it about attempted suicide. Neither suicide nor attempted suicide is considered a criminal act. Instead, the current debate is about whether public policy should be changed in a way that will transform prescriptions for poison into "medical treatment."

Oregon and Beyond

Oregon is the only place in the world with a specific law permitting assisted suicide. (Although widely practiced in the Netherlands, euthanasia and assisted suicide remain technically illegal in that country.) Unfortunately, there is no way to know of abuses, or even the number of deaths, occurring under the Oregon law, since failure to adhere to its reporting requirements is not penalized.

But we do know that in Oregon a doctor can write a prescription for drugs that are intended to kill the patient. When the prescription is filled, the pharmacist doesn't give the usual instructions about how to take it safely. Instead, a patient is more likely to hear, "Be sure to take all of these pills at one time—with a light snack or alcohol—to induce death." Directions center around making certain that the patient dies after taking the prescription.

Reprinted from Rita L. Marker, Symposium: "Should Physician-Assisted Suicide Be Legalized by the States? No: Accepting Physician-Assisted Suicide Would Lead America Down a Cold, Cruel Path," *Insight*, March 8, 1999, by permission of *Insight* magazine. Copyright ©1999 by News World Communications, Inc. All rights reserved.

The lethal drugs are covered by some Oregon health-insurance plans. They are paid for by the state Medicaid program under a funding category called "comfort care." (This certainly gives meaning to the statement, "All social engineering is preceded by verbal engineering.") Even though Oregon stands alone in approving such so-called comfort care, there is a full-court press to expand its legalization to every state. Already Hawaii's governor has vowed to propose legalization of both euthanasia as well as assisted suicide. A court

> *"The least costly treatment for any illness is lethal medication."*

challenge to Alaska's law prohibiting assisted suicide has been filed. Attempts to place the issue on the ballot have begun in several states. And, in virtually every state, there is a lawmaker who is drafting an assisted-suicide proposal.

Publicity Stunts

Assisted-suicide activists expect many of these efforts to fail initially but count on their providing the opportunity for publicity. This publicity follows a rarely altered pattern. First, a "hard case" is spotlighted. This is accompanied by the assertion that assisted suicide was a necessary last resort. Assurances are made that the method and timing of death were freely chosen by the person (who is, conveniently, dead and thus unable to refute these claims). Finally, accusations are made that anyone who dares raise questions about such a demise lacks compassion and merely wants to force others to suffer.

It should be noted that many advocates of assisted suicide seriously believe that what they're proposing is a compassionate choice that should be available. However, despite their sincerity and good intent, it is the content, not the intent, of the policies and laws they espouse that ultimately will affect each and every person.

Whether other states embrace Oregon-style "comfort care" will depend upon a willingness to carefully examine what truly is at stake in this debate. This is, above all, a debate about public policy.

The Power of Cost Containment

No matter what one's views may be about the concept of assisted suicide, it's necessary to reflect on the context in which it would be carried out. This reflection necessarily includes consideration of contemporary economic forces affecting health care. As acting solicitor general Walter Dellinger said during his 1997 argument against assisted suicide before the U.S. Supreme Court, "The least costly treatment for any illness is lethal medication." He was, of course, correct. A prescription for a deadly overdose runs about $35. Once taken, the patient won't consume any more health-care dollars.

Cost containment well could become the engine that pulls the legislative train along the track to death on demand. Those who advocate dismantling the barriers that now protect patients from assisted suicide recognize the power of cost containment. For example, Hemlock Society cofounder Derek Humphry recently explained his belief that, in the final analysis, economics will drive assisted suicide to the plateau of acceptable practice.

The Changing Economics of Health Care

There's no question that economic considerations always have played a role in decisions about health care. Most of us can recall a time not long ago when patients routinely were subjected to unneeded tests and treatments. And we know now that money fueled these abuses. Then, health providers were reimbursed for everything they did to or for a patient.

Fortunately, patients and families became more aware of their rights to reject unwanted and unnecessary interventions. But the end to overtreatment didn't stem primarily from a respect for patients' rights. Instead, it grew out of changes in the way health care is reimbursed.

No longer do doctors and hospitals get paid for all they do. Instead, their incomes often depend upon how little they provide. And now, not surprisingly, the pendulum has swung to the other extreme, where more and more people (insured and uninsured alike) find it difficult, if not impossible, to get needed and wanted health care. Again, the fuel for change is money. The catalyst has been managed care.

For-Profit Medicine

Managed care has dominated health-care delivery in recent years. A significant number of health-maintenance organizations, or HMOs, are "for-profit" enterprises where stockholder benefit, not patient well-being, is the bottom line. Gatekeepers operate to protect resources by delaying or denying authorization for services.

Some programs have what are called "gag rules," which prohibit doctors from telling patients the whole truth about interventions that might be helpful. The stark words, "There's nothing that can be done" may really mean, "There's nothing more we'll pay for." But patients may not know that.

Imagine the patient who is in pain and is given the "nothing can be done" routine. Pain control definitely is given short shrift by many health plans. Some plans don't provide coverage for chronic pain except in very limited circumstances. Others put an unreasonably low cap on the amount paid for hospice care. (One Oregon insurer limits payment for hospice care to a $1,000 maximum.)

> *"The stark words, 'There's nothing that can be done' may really mean, 'There's nothing more we'll pay for.'"*

Navigating the murky health-insurance waters of services not covered, services not approved and the complex methods of copayments is particularly difficult for patients who are seriously ill and/or in pain. They have precious little energy to deal with a system that seems impenetrable.

Few people pay much attention to the particulars of their health-insurance coverage until they are ill. By then it may be too late. Assisted-suicide advocates assure us that a physician only would prescribe the lethal overdose after careful discussion with the patient.

To make this assertion represents the height of naïveté, if not disingenuousness. It's a presumption made by those relatively few people who have the luxury of a personal family physician who also may be a golfing or bridge partner.

Having a physician friend who would talk over a planned assisted suicide before prescribing a lethal dose is nothing more than a fantasy for the vast majority of Americans.

> *"Having a physician friend who would talk over a planned assisted suicide before prescribing a lethal dose is nothing more than a fantasy for . . . [most] Americans."*

Today most people are fortunate if they see the same doctor from visit to visit and, even when they do, time constraints exist. For example, some managed-care programs expect physicians to limit new-patient visits to 20 minutes and are told to devote no more than 10 minutes to a returning patient. Do we really believe that health plans that limit doctors' time in this manner would let doctors spend hours discussing the pros and cons of assisted suicide before prescribing the fatal dose?

Physicians' Incentives to Encourage Suicide

Conflicts of interest also should be recognized. An obvious concern is the possibility that a physician could persuasively "offer" the option of assisted suicide to a patient whom the physician knows may pose the threat of a malpractice case. But there are more subtle, more likely, types of competing interests between physicians and patients. For instance, some health programs provide financial bonuses to doctors who conserve economic resources by withholding time or care from patients. It's reasonable to point out that this has the potential for conflicts of interest between patients and physicians.

Add to this the results of a survey published in 1998 in the *Archives of Internal Medicine*. It found that doctors who are the most thrifty when it comes to medical expenses would be six times more likely than their counterparts to provide a lethal prescription. These same doctors would be diagnosing, screening and counseling patients—and prescribing lethal drugs for assisted suicide.

Comfort Care Is Not Really an Option

Even in light of such concerns, activists favoring assisted suicide contend that the choice of assisted suicide should be available. Choice is meaningless, however, if there is only one affordable option. True, advocates of assisted suicide insist that every person, prior to receiving assisted suicide, would be offered all options. This appears protective. But there is a vast difference between an offer of something and the ability to accept that offer. This difference was acknowledged at a conference in which assisted-suicide guidelines, drafted by a San Francisco ethics committee, were under discussion. The guidelines stated that physicians had to offer palliative care (pain and symptom management) to patients before providing assisted suicide. However, when asked if there was also a mandate that patients have actual access to this care before being given a lethal prescription, the ethics-committee spokesperson replied that there was no such requirement.

Thus, the offer of all options is grossly misleading. It creates the illusion that all options would be available to people when, in fact, they would not. In theory, offering the choices between unaffordable palliative care and an affordable drug overdose is one thing. In practice, it takes little imagination to figure out which "choice" is really available. As attorney and consumer advocate Wesley Smith has said, "The last people to receive medical care will be the first to receive assisted suicide." If we embrace assisted suicide as medical treatment, it will return our embrace with a death grip that is cold, cruel and anything but compassionate.

Chapter 2

What Ethics Should Guide Organ Transplants?

CURRENT CONTROVERSIES

The Ethics of Organ Transplants: An Overview

by Karen K. Giuliano

About the author: *Karen K. Giuliano is a registered nurse and a contributor to* Nursing *magazine.*

Editor's note: The following overview was originally intended for nurses and other medical personnel.

As organ transplantation becomes easier to do, the ethical questions become harder to answer.

When you care for patients who could benefit from a transplant, you'll be drawn into conflicts that have no easy solutions. Here, we'll explore some of the most nettlesome issues surrounding organ transplantation so you can help patients and their families make sound decisions.

As of January 1997, 50,288 people were on the national waiting list for a donor organ. Most of them will die waiting.

No Easy Answers

Because of spectacular medical advances, the successful transplantation of vital organs—notably the heart, liver, and kidney—has become routine at many medical centers. Patients facing death are restored to health; many can expect to live a near-normal life span.

Ironically, our success at organ transplantation has opened a Pandora's box of ethical questions involving the allocation of scarce donor organs. For example, should an organ go to the sickest patient on the waiting list, or to a more robust patient who may live longer? . . . Is taking a kidney from a living donor ethical? If so, should living donors be compensated for the lost organ—as blood donors may be for blood?

These and other questions surrounding organ transplantation have no easy answers and continue to be the subject of public controversy. As you care for patients who may be candidates for transplantation—and family members who are

Adapted, with permission, from K.K. Giuliano, "Organ Transplants: Tackling the Tough Ethical Questions," *Nursing97*, vol. 27, no. 5, pp. 34–39; © Springhouse Corporation.

potential living donors—you'll be drawn into the debate. In this article, I'll explore some of these issues and offer insights that you can share with your patients.

Should a Patient's Relatives Be Permitted to Donate a Kidney?

Approximately 25% of the transplanted kidneys in this country come from living donors; by far, most of these donors are related by blood to the recipient. Before a transplant involving a living donor occurs, several conditions should be met. First, the donation must not impair the donor's life or health. Second, the donation must be completely voluntary. Finally, all risks should be fully explained.

Obtaining a kidney from a living donor has some clear advantages for the patient:

- The results are generally better with living-donor kidneys than with those obtained from cadavers. For example, a living-donor kidney has a better chance of immediate postoperative function. With cadaveric transplants, a period of cold ischemia [during which the body's blood flow ceases and no oxygen reaches the organ] heightens the risk of postoperative acute tubular necrosis (ATN). Although ATN usually resolves, it makes the postoperative course much more unpredictable.
- A patient receiving a kidney from a relative won't have to wait on the national list for a suitable kidney to become available.
- The surgery can be performed as a planned elective procedure under optimal conditions.

"Our success at organ transplantation has opened a Pandora's box of ethical questions involving the allocation of scarce donor organs."

But what about the risks to the donor? Statistically, serious complications following unilateral nephrectomy [kidney removal] are rare. After the nephrectomy, the donor's renal function rapidly returns to approximately 90% of the preoperative baseline. Although losing a kidney causes a slight functional decline, the deficit is clinically insignificant.

Nevertheless, the surgery is painful—generally more painful than surgery to implant a kidney—and recovery for the donor may be longer and more complicated than for the recipient. And while the donation may not affect the donor's health at first, it will have serious consequences if disease or an injury impairs his remaining kidney later in life.

Is it ethical to expose a healthy donor to any risk for a procedure that won't benefit him and could cause harm? Many practitioners believe the answer is no.

An Emotional Issue

You also have to consider psychological issues and family dynamics. I once cared for a woman who donated a kidney to her brother. After surgery, he didn't follow his medication schedule and, as a result, the donated kidney was rejected. The man's sister felt a good deal of resentment toward her brother because, in her eyes, she'd given a precious gift and he hadn't respected it enough to take care of it.

You could argue that many living donors benefit emotionally when they help a relative by donating an organ. But it would be naive to believe that coercion never occurs. In a recent interview, prominent medical bioethicist Art Caplan said he believes telling "small lies" can be ethical and even necessary to prevent a patient or other relatives from pressuring a potential donor.

> *"Because of the potential for psychological and physical harm, some surgeons refuse to perform transplants involving living donors."*

"With kidney donation, I began having questions on the way we were counseling family members who'd been called upon to donate live organs," Caplan told a writer from the *New York Times*. "I realized family ties could be coercive. So I went in and talked to our transplant team and said: 'Before we accept any more live kidney donations, we'd better be prepared to give people a medical excuse, lie for them—so they feel they don't have to withstand the wrath of their family if they say no to having someone cut them up and take one of their kidneys.' And I got a guy right away who, when offered the chance, said no to donating to his brother."

No doubt many reluctant donors are motivated by guilt—but guilt can cut both ways. I was once involved in the care of a man who'd received a kidney from his wife. His surgery went well and he recovered quickly without complications. His wife, however, had a difficult postoperative course; during her extended hospital stay, her husband helped care for her, which was a role reversal because she'd always cared for him. The husband experienced enormous guilt over his wife's discomfort.

Because of the potential for psychological and physical harm, some surgeons refuse to perform transplants involving living donors. But standards and policies vary among transplant centers—and even among practitioners at the same center.

Should Donors Be Compensated for Their Organs?

The 1984 National Organ Transplant Act makes selling organs illegal in the United States. Some people think this policy should be reconsidered, for some fairly compelling reasons:

- Offering compensation would encourage donation, increasing the number of organs available.
- Everyone else involved in the transplant process is compensated. Why not the donor or his family?
- We live in a free-market society. Why shouldn't an individual be permitted to do what he wishes with his own valuable organs?

People opposed to compensating donors would answer the last question by pointing to the potential for black-market commerce. In fact, many argue that just by accepting living-donor organs, we've already stepped onto that slippery slope. . . .

To encourage organ donation without promoting black-market activity, some experts in the transplant field have suggested legalizing and strictly regulating limited forms of compensation. They point out that although the recipient's insurance generally pays for expenses associated with the procedure, the donor's lost work time may not be compensated under current policies.

Another proposal is to pay family members a death benefit for cadaver organs. This compensation would be a standard amount administered according to uniform rules. But that proposal raises a host of new questions and controversies. Could the possibility of a death benefit tempt relatives to consent to a donation that the donor himself wouldn't have agreed to? And if relatives can benefit from a donor's organs after the donor's death, why shouldn't people have the option of selling their own organs before death and benefiting themselves?

Problems with Selling Organs

On the other hand, might families feel uncomfortable accepting payment for a loved one's body parts? If so, obtaining consent for organ donation could become more, not less, difficult.

Other societies wrestle with the compensation issue too. In the United Kingdom, for example, selling organs is illegal, and only under special conditions do patients receive organs from living donors who aren't blood relatives.

However, selling organs is legal in many countries, including Turkey, Brazil, Japan, Egypt, Iraq, and the Philippines. Until recently, the practice was also legal in India, but the law was changed in response to social problems the practice engendered. Between 1990 and 1995, more than 2,000 kidneys were sold annually to wealthy Middle Eastern recipients. At that rate, many of the poorest people in India would have been minus a kidney by the year 2000.

"The 1984 National Organ Transplant Act makes selling organs illegal in the United States. Some people think this policy should be reconsidered."

Typically, these donors were extremely poor, not necessarily healthy, and in desperate need of money for survival. Many eventually found themselves worse off than before—still poor, but now ill and debilitated too. Under those circumstances, can organ donation truly be considered free and uncoerced?

Do Animal Transplants Offer a Realistic Alternative?

Xenografting—transplanting tissue between two different species—shows promise in several areas. Injecting islet cells from genetically engineered pigs into the hepatic circulation or abdominal cavity, for example, could reduce the need for pancreas transplantation, which is technically difficult. Using primates or even genetically engineered pigs for heart transplantation may also be scientifically possible.

But the ethical and practical barriers are formidable. When we consider using xenotransplantation, we need to ask these questions: What's the difference between killing animals for food and killing them for xenotransplantation? Is it acceptable to kill only certain animals for transplantable tissues? How will these animals be treated before death? What kind of psychological problems might a recipient face if his human heart is replaced with an ape's?

> *"Selling organs is legal in many countries."*

Many of us could accept procuring tissue from pigs. But are we willing to condone the routine procuring of organs from our fellow primates?

Besides ethical considerations, practical problems exist—for example, primates are difficult to breed in captivity, so the few organs we'd obtain probably wouldn't make much of a dent in the current shortage.

Finally, consider the real risk of transmitting animal diseases to human hosts. Animal diseases that can be transmitted to humans include rabies and strains of the Ebola virus. The danger is especially high when the human host is immunosuppressed (as most organ transplant patients must be) and the donor is a genetically similar primate.

To address this issue, the federal Public Health Service issued xenotransplant guidelines in September 1996. Covering a range of xenotransplant therapies, the guidelines call on researchers to carefully screen animals for disease, preserve blood and tissue samples from the donor animal, and monitor patients for emerging diseases. . . .

Is the Current Organ Allocation Program Fair?

Deciding which patients on the waiting list should get priority . . . is also controversial. In the United States, UNOS [United Network for Organ Sharing] maintains a national waiting list for organs. In general, the sickest patients routinely move to the top of the list.

In a controversial policy change, UNOS shifted its position on this issue for liver transplants in late 1996. Under the new policy, patients suffering from acute failure would get priority over those with long-term liver failure, because they have a better chance of full recovery. In March 1997, however, UNOS put the new policy on hold pending further review. . . .

Allocating organs according to medical urgency remains the general policy for all organs. (However, this criterion plays a lesser role in kidney transplantation because most patients can be sustained indefinitely with dialysis.) Although intended to be as fair and unbiased as possible, the policy has flaws that can give some patients an unfair advantage.

For example, UNOS maintains a national list, but organs are distributed regionally whenever possible. This is both cost-effective and medically sound because limiting the time an organ is preserved enhances its viability.

But that means a patient can improve his odds of receiving an organ by getting himself listed at more than one transplant center; he may have a better chance at a distant center simply because its list is shorter. So a wealthy patient who can afford to travel to several centers will probably get an organ faster than a patient who can't. [The Department of Health and Human Services has pressed for a nationally coordinated system of organ allocation to eliminate unfair geographic distribution, but as of March 1999 the plan has not been implemented.]

What's more, a patient can be on waiting lists for more than one organ. Many people question the fairness of giving one person more than one organ when so many are waiting for just one.

This issue was publicized in 1994 when Pennsylvania Governor Bob Casey received a heart and liver transplant after spending virtually no time on the waiting list. Many people were outraged over what appeared to be a public figure's unfair access to donated organs.

At the time, UNOS maintained a separate list for combined transplants. Today, however, people needing two organs are placed on the list for each organ. They get priority when they reach the top of either list.

When a patient needs two organs, his chance of survival is best if both organs are taken from the same donor. So, depending on the urgency of his condition, he may take priority over two other patients waiting for the same organs.

Animal-to-Human Transplants Could Save Lives

by David White, interviewed by Cory SerVaas

About the author: *David White is cofounder and research director of Imutran, a biotechnology company based in the United Kingdom.*

Edward Jenner ran into resistance when he first tried to popularize smallpox inoculation because the vaccine he used was derived from cows. Opponents to the lifesaving inoculation published derisive cartoons of children with cows' horns growing from their heads. Today, researchers are running into a similar problem trying to expedite the use of pig organs for human transplantation.

The Potential to Save Countless Lives

At this moment, over 50,000 people are on the national waiting list for an organ transplant, yet most won't receive one. Nearly 10 people die each day waiting and hoping for a lifesaving organ. And the need for organ transplants will only grow as the baby boom population ages. But advances in genetic engineering are offering a solution. Dr. David White of the biotechnology company Imutran in Cambridge, England, has been trying to reduce this critical shortage of organs using organs of genetically engineered pigs, suitable for transplantation into humans. The science of transplanting organs across species is called xenotransplantation. In the future, Dr. White's "transgenic" pigs will be produced by injecting the future pig's embryonic egg with the human recipient's DNA. The dreaded organ rejection will thus be avoided because the host's immune system would not recognize the customized pig organ as foreign material. The immune system would recognize the organ not just as a human heart, but as the patient's own heart. Surgery can be scheduled as soon as the pig is ready.

"The nice thing about the pig is you know who the donor is going to be weeks or months before the transplant," Dr. White said. "It's not like you're waiting for someone to fall off his motorcycle."

The Use of Animals to Save Human Lives Is Not New

For decades, medicine has been relying on animals in saving human lives. Insulin from the pancreas of pigs has kept diabetics alive; pig valves have been successfully used to replace damaged valves in cardiac patients, and pig skin has helped save burn victims. (We consume some 90 million pigs each year.)

Dr. White's research has brought us to the threshold at which pig organs—such as lungs, livers, and hearts—can be used to save the lives of people dying for lack of a human donor transplant.

We invited Dr. White to dinner and attended his seminars at the Indiana University School of Medicine.

Cory SerVaas: *When did you begin researching the use of pig organs for transplants?*

David White: We have been very concerned over the lack of organs for transplantation for 10 or 12 years. To combat the problem, we've been genetically engineering pigs so that they now can provide hearts and kidneys for transplantation into patients.

> *"We've been genetically engineering pigs so that they now can provide hearts and kidneys for transplantation into patients."*

We've been able to demonstrate that we can transplant pig hearts and pig kidneys into monkeys without the rejection process that is normally associated with that kind of transplantation.

We're excited that we now have developed a new lifesaving therapy that can be applied to hundreds and thousands of people across the world. But we do have the duty to make sure that this process is safe.

Obstacles to Overcome

What about the fear of some new viral infection?

There is a concern that there may be some unknown virus in pigs that will get into the human population and cause a new epidemic as a result of the transplant. We've spent the past year—and intend to spend a lot more time—to show people that there is absolutely no worry at all as far as the possibility of a pig virus is concerned. We've developed protocols that allow us to breed pigs in an environment where we can eliminate any known pathogens. But, to be quite frank, people have been exchanging bodily fluids with pigs for millennia, if you think about pig farmers or slaughtermen who cut their fingers while butchering pigs. So we don't believe that there's anything out there that is not known. Furthermore, we think the fact that man and pig have been associated closely for so many millennia is good evidence that there are no unknown antigens in pigs to affect man.

What, then, is preventing you from transplanting pig organs into people?

Well, the problem that we currently face is that we have these pigs, and people will say, "Yes, you can transplant them into your patients if you know it's safe."

But how do we know it's safe if we can't transplant them into our patients? In order to get around that, we've been doing studies transplanting these hearts and kidneys into

> *"There is absolutely no worry at all as far as the possibility of a pig virus is concerned."*

monkeys. We can now demonstrate it is safe for the monkeys. Of course, our opponents will say, "Yes, but even though it's safe for the monkeys, how do you know it's safe for human beings? We can't let you transplant into humans until you've made it safe for human beings."

So what we are trying to do is move sideways, as it were. Our first clinical trials will be using livers of pigs, not as a transplant but as a bridge to liver transplantation in which we can pump the patient's blood through the pig liver and keep them alive until a human liver becomes available, or possibly until their own liver recovers.

Success Is Imminent

Your company has joined with the pharmaceutical giant Novartis [which produces the drug cyclosporin, an immunosuppressant that is vital to the success of organ transplant operations]. How will this help your research efforts?

In the development of new technologies such as genetically engineering pigs: first of all, clearly, it's a very high-risk business. Secondly, it's a very expensive business, so that you need to have a very wealthy backup who is prepared to take the long-term view. It's really only the large pharmaceutical companies such as Novartis who are able to support what potentially could revolutionize medical care. So the Novartis support for our research program is absolutely critical.

How soon do you think you could be transplanting pig organs?

I would be very disappointed if we don't start our transplantation program before the end of the millennium. [Here he exudes confidence!]

If a baby receives a pig heart, do you believe the pig heart will grow as the baby grows, or might you have to transplant a larger heart later?

It's almost certainly the case that these organs will grow as demand is put upon them. In the monkeys, the kidneys of pigs grow to about twice the size that you would expect. But of course, that's because the monkey would normally have two kidneys. So we believe that growth is demand-driven, that organs grow to support the level that you want.

The Only Option for Many

What do people on the transplant waiting list think about this alternative?

Well, you know, you can be as philosophical as you like about death. The fact of the matter is, most people would rather be alive than dead, and if you say that you can be dead in three months or you can have a pig-heart transplant with a risk that in 20 years you might get leukemia, there are no choices. It's an option other than death.

In the United States, nine out of ten people die waiting for organ transplants.

It's the same everywhere. Transplantation currently for the treatment of heart failure is an entirely peripheral activity. The numbers of heart transplants we do don't even begin to reflect the number of deaths from coronary disease.

Transplantation is a direct reflection on the number of donors. If you look at the United Kingdom, we will produce about 13 donors per million of population per annum. In the U.S., you produce about 21 donors per million of population per annum. Actually, the best country in the world is Spain, with 29 donors per million per annum. The problem is, for the transplantation to be a successful therapy, it's not 29 donors per million we need, it's 290, maybe 2,900. If you just look at the figures in the United States, it's been conservatively estimated that you need to do about 100,000 transplants a year. Last year you had just under 6,000 donors. For 100,000 transplants you have 6,000 donors. The equation doesn't add up.

Pigs Are the Answer

What can [individuals] do to help?

There are several important things that they could do. Xenotransplantation is in a very early stage. We hope to start clinical trials, perhaps at the end of this year, perhaps early next year. So, the first thing I'd ask them to do is to continue supporting current organ-donation processes. The second thing I would ask is that they think very carefully about the way organ donation is now and the way it could be if xenotransplantation becomes a reality—how many more lives we could save—and that they support us as we introduce this kind of model technology (which is perhaps a little bit frightening) in a calm, sensible, safe, stepwise approach.

Pigs are the answer?

I think pigs will be the obvious solution.

Animal-to-Human Transplants Are Dangerous and Unethical

by Alan Berger and Gil Lamont

About the author: *Alan Berger is executive director and Gil Lamont is senior editor of* Animal Issues, *the magazine of the Animal Protection Institute, a non-profit organization that advocates the humane treatment of all animals.*

More than at any time in history, many of us today have the opportunity to live longer and healthier lives. Significant advances in immunosuppression and other techniques have greatly increased the success of human-to-human transplants ("allografts") to replace worn-out body organs. Too bad there aren't enough body parts to go around.

Despite encouraging organ donors—even the Department of Health and Human Services has a web site devoted to the issue at "http://www.organdonor.gov"—the number of waiting recipients is climbing steadily. In 1988, the United Network for Organ Sharing (UNOS) listed 16,026 registrants waiting for transplants. In 1998, the list numbers nearly 55,000.

The number of donor organs, although increasing, has not kept pace. The pesky lack of donors has the medical community looking longingly at xenografts (animal-to-human transplants) as the perfect answer.

Even when we put aside the serious ethical considerations of using animals as walking containers of spare parts, there are serious financial and health consequences to xenografts.

An Expensive Innovation

The wholesale adoption of xenotransplants, using organs from genetically altered pigs, will generate enormous profits for the pharmaceutical industry, for the bioengineering firms that supply the pigs, and for the medical professionals involved.

Reprinted from Alan Berger and Gil Lamont, "Plunging Headlong into Madness," *Animal Issues*, Summer 1998, by permission of the Animal Protection Institute, www.api4animals.org. (The extensive notes in the original have been omitted in this reprint.)

"Xenotransplantation," reports one story, "could become a $3 billion to $5 billion a year business within the next dozen years."

Good for industry, bad for the consumer. Already 40 million Americans are uninsured, increasing to 48 million—by 20%—by the year 2000. Another 29 million are underinsured.

Meanwhile, health care costs are skyrocketing. We spend $425 billion a year—about two-thirds of all medical expenditures—to treat the six leading chronic diseases that cause nearly three-quarters of all deaths: heart disease, cancer, stroke, diabetes, chronic obstructive pulmonary disease, and liver disease.

> *"Xenotransplant proponents have already begun a carefully orchestrated education of the public to accept xenografts."*

Current transplant costs range from $116,000 for a kidney to more than $300,000 for a liver. Factoring in five years of follow-up charges puts the costs at nearly $400,000 for a liver transplant, with heart, heart-lung, and lung transplants totaling more than $300,000 each. Adding xenografts to allografts will boost annual transplant expenditures from nearly $3 billion to $20.3 billion. And it can only rise from there.

An Unfair, Inadequate Health Care System

Meanwhile, people's confidence in our health care system is dwindling. In a National Coalition on Health Care poll, 80% believe something is "seriously wrong" with the system and 87% that the quality of care needs to be improved. Eight of 10 blamed the profit motive for compromising quality.

"In these times of managed care and a nationwide glut of hospital beds," reported the *Wall Street Journal* on the reluctance of state officials to authorize $300 million to overhaul an aging hospital in Brooklyn, "reviving [these ailing medical centers] may make little economic sense. Experts say it is time for a better way: lean clinics that provide out-patient and primary care."

But when health care management takes services away from poorer neighborhoods, the "nationwide glut of hospital beds" is not available to the people who need them most, as revealed in a new study by the Harvard University School of Public Health. There's virtually no access to health care for native Americans on reservations, for urban blacks, for the poor concentrated anywhere. For them, health is poorer, life is shorter. Health care access can vary life expectancies by as much as 15 years between areas as little apart as 12 miles.

Skewed Priorities

In a 1993 Kaiser/Commonwealth Fund health insurance survey, 34% of the uninsured reported that they failed to receive needed care, and 71% postponed needed care. And the uninsured who have chronic illnesses "are least likely to receive proper maintenance and continuous care, with the result that untreated conditions such as hypertension or diabetes can lead to serious health consequences."

Instead of allocating health costs to providing care to the millions who can't get it, our "baby boomer" bias concentrates on keeping that aging population bulge alive. Xenotransplant proponents have already begun a carefully orchestrated education of the public to accept xenografts, as evidenced by a recent press release: "Nearly all Americans (94%) are aware of the shortage of available organs for transplant and most (62%) accept the concept of xenotransplantation, or animal-to-human transplantation, as a viable option." And "nearly 75 percent of people in all the groups surveyed would consider a xenotransplant for a loved one if the organ or tissue were unavailable from a human."

Diseases That Can Jump Between Species

Evidently these people don't have all the facts. Certain diseases jump from animals to humans (zoonosis). The best known example is probably AIDS, which even Centers for Disease Control (CDC) scientists now acknowledge "resulted from the adaptation of simian retroviruses introduced across species lines into humans." The historically best known example is that of the 1918 influenza epidemic, which killed more than 20 million people worldwide and is now believed to have been a mutated swine virus carried to Europe by U.S. troops.

Nor are these isolated examples. Recently health officials in Hong Kong destroyed millions of chickens after a virus, A(H5N1), jumped directly from the birds to humans. And lately there has been much publicity over the occurrence of Creutzfeldt-Jakob disease (CJD), a fatal brain-wasting illness that has claimed a number of British humans' lives and which has been linked to mad cow disease (bovine spongiform encephalopathy).

> *"Breeding virus-free pigs will be extremely difficult, if not impossible."*

The animal of choice for supplying xenotransplant organs is the pig. The transgenic pigs will be raised in a sterile environment, but pigs bring a whole new set of problems to the issue of xenosis (viruses transmitted during xenotransplants).

No Getting Away from Viruses

Recent findings by London researchers—at the Institute of Cancer Research and the National Institute of Medical Research (NIMR)—suggest that breeding virus-free pigs will be extremely difficult, if not impossible.

Sensitive molecular probes searched pigs from a range of breeds for copies of two inherited retroviruses, PERV-A and PERV-B (porcine endogenous proviruses), which can infect human cells. All the pigs tested possessed multiple copies of the viruses, 10–23 copies of the PERV-A genes and 7–12 copies of PERV-B genes.

"The existence of 20 to 30 copies per cell will make it very much harder to remove the viruses from pig cells," said Dr. Jonathan P. Stoye of the NIMR, who led the research. "It may actually be impossible."

In the lab both viruses infect human cells, but nobody will commit to whether they will cause disease in people. Dr. Stoye, who wants further investigation before proceeding with pig-to-human xenotransplants, says, "We ought to know more about the pathogenic potential of these viruses."

We do know that humans can already acquire approximately 25 diseases from pigs, including anthrax, influenza, scabies, rabies, leptospirosis (which produces liver and kidney damage) and erysipclas (a skin infection).

The Dangers Are Unknown

Despite the above recognition that the dangers are unknown; despite the federal government's own assessment that the risk of infection cannot be quantified ("unequivocally greater than zero" was the official position); despite the requests of leading scientists that a moratorium be imposed on clinical xenotransplantation "in the public interest"; the government is committed to xenotransplantation.

At a December 1997 meeting, the Xenotransplant Advisory Subcommittee of the U.S. Food and Drug Administration (FDA) recommended that the FDA approve "limited" human clinical trials for xenotransplantation.

"Developing U.S. Public Health Service [PHS] Policy in Xenotransplantation," a January 1998 government-sponsored conference announced the imminent release of final PHS Guidelines for Xenotransplantation to Protect Against Infectious Diseases. The oversight agency for xenotransplantation will be the FDA.

The government intends to protect the public through cumbersome procedures that include screening donor animals for known viruses, constant surveillance of xenotransplant recipients and their contacts, maintaining tissue and blood samples from donor animals and human recipients, and establishing national and local registries of xenograft patients.

Given the scope of xenotransplants expected, the number of patients will, most likely, quickly outstrip the capabilities of the necessary database. As for screening for known viruses, what about the unknown ones? In February 1998, Australian scientists discovered an unknown virus in pigs. It apparently came from a colony of fruitbats that lived nearby. Once it hit the piggery the virus attacked pig fetuses, which were either stillborn or had defects in the spinal cord and brain. It also infected two human workers, who recovered. "You can't screen for disease agents that you don't know about," said virologist Peter Kirkland.

"Prevention . . . is much less expensive and far more effective [than transplantation]."

And after the virus is discovered, what can we really do about it? HIV has been known for decades, yet worldwide the AIDS epidemic is getting worse.

Increasing the Number of Human Donors

Would xenografts even be an option if enough human donor organs were available? Recent advances point the way to greater compatibility of organ and recipient. The discoverer of a "facilitating cell" that helps stem cells engraft says that "universal organ transplants may be possible, which may alleviate the chronic shortage of organs."

That "chronic shortage" may also be reduced by a new National Organ and Tissue Donor Initiative, and new policies in several states. Beginning in 1995, Pennsylvania hospitals are required to notify the regional organ procurement organization upon each patient's death to determine potential for organ or tissue donation. This immediately increased referrals tenfold. An aggressive education program has also increased public awareness of the need for donors, especially for people renewing their driver licenses; in the first year, more than 820,000 drivers chose to have "organ donor" printed on the front of their licenses beneath their photograph. Similar legislation has been enacted or is being considered in New Jersey, Maryland, and other states.

> *"We cannot continue to cure human lives by the wholesale taking of animal lives."*

While applauding all efforts to encourage more people to become organ donors, the Animal Protection Institute (API) supports enacting a national Presumed Consent Law, which supports a growing majority of Americans expressing a willingness to donate their organs at death. This law would assume that, *unless expressed otherwise before death*, everyone is a potential organ donor upon his or her demise. (Provisions for minors and the infirm require parental or guardian consent.) An opposite wish may simply be communicated in writing.

A Better Way

While transplants may offer longer and healthier lives to the chronically ill, one form of "medicine" reigns supreme. "I really don't think transplantation is going to be the answer," says Charles Porter, a Missouri cardiologist. "It's going to rehabilitation and prevention." Rep. Jim Moran, D-Va., agrees, pointing out that the nation spends far too much on curing illnesses and not enough trying to prevent them. "Prevention," he says, "is much less expensive and far more effective."

Indeed, most illnesses are preventable. Changes in diet and increasing exercise can reduce high blood pressure, heart attacks, and cancer. Yet most people behave as if their bodies are machines to be worn out, or that the medical community sees transgenic pigs as the mobile warehouses for spare parts. Of the enormous numbers of dollars spent on health care, only a fraction goes to prevention and control efforts—about 3% of most state public health departments' budgets. In 1994, over $287 million was spent at the state level on prevention efforts aimed at the six leading chronic diseases (heart disease, cancer, stroke, diabetes, chronic obstructive pulmonary disease, and chronic liver disease). This was approximately 0.07% of the estimated $425 billion spent annually to treat those same diseases, according to a CDC study.

Xenotransplantation is not the answer, despite all the rosy pictures overoptimistic researchers, genetic engineers, and pharmaceutical companies, paint of readily available organs. Since 1994, API has been saying exactly that, in a series of position papers, arguments, and at government-sponsored conferences. We cannot continue to cure human lives by the wholesale taking of animal lives. We cannot continue to deny health care to others simply because where they live prevents that health care from being "cost effective." We must learn to take better care of each other, by becoming organ donors, and better care of ourselves, through diet and exercise.

Commerce in Organs Is Ethical

by Leonard Lu

About the author: *Leonard Lu is a graduate of the Brown University School of Medicine and is currently conducting research at Harvard Medical School.*

The limited supply of cadaveric kidneys coupled with an increasing demand for transplantable kidneys has forced the medical community to examine novel methods of organ procurement. Specifically, there are only about 10,000 cadaveric kidneys available for the 200,000 end-stage renal [kidney] disease (ESRD) patients in the United States. This shortage is compounded by the fact that the number of donors has plateaued, while the number of ESRD patients has grown at a rate of 8–9 percent per year. This trend is likely to continue so long as diseases such as diabetes mellitus remain incurable. One controversial approach for increasing the supply of kidneys is to implement a system of commerce in organ transplantation. The idea is simple: if only one kidney is necessary to sustain renal function, why not sell the other? In various parts of the world, the sale of kidneys is exactly what is happening. In 1989, a case that gained international attention involved a Turkish peasant who was flown to London to donate a kidney, for approximately $4,400. The United Kingdom, the United States, and other developed nations, however, have explicitly outlawed the sale of organs. In support of U.S. policy, the Committee on Morals and Ethics of the Transplantation Society has asserted, "The sale of organs by donors living or dead is indefensible under any circumstances."

In the first part of this viewpoint, I argue in favor of commerce in kidney transplantation by showing that such a practice is consistent with current ethical standards in medicine. Then, in the second part, I assume (for the sake of the argument) that the sale of kidneys is acceptable, in order to create a framework for a hypothetical organ commerce policy.

The Body as Property

The first argument in favor of the sale of kidneys is the notion of the "body as property." If the body is considered property, then the transfer of body parts is protected under the rights of owner- ship. Critics of this approach point out, however, that the human body is protected under "quasi-property rights." Under this doctrine, the hu- man body is classified as a special

> *"If only one kidney is necessary to sustain renal function, why not sell the other?"*

form of property that deserves limited property rights. This concept provokes the following question: "If we sell (or permit the sale of) other goods, why not organs, and if we transfer (or permit the transfer of) organs in other ways, why not by sales?" For example, if it is acceptable to sell blood plasma and sperm, why not a kidney? Opponents of organ commerce argue that kidneys are nonre- generative organs, and hence differ significantly from other donor parts. On the other hand, proponents of organ commerce bring forth libertarian and utilitarian arguments. The former relies on the principle of autonomy, and states that indi- viduals should be allowed to do whatever they please with their bodies, includ- ing selling a kidney. The latter maintains that happiness can be maximized un- der a system of commerce (that is, it is the most effective means of increasing the organ supply). Further, as intended under a capitalist system, both the buyer and seller gain utility from the transaction—in this case, the buyer receives a kidney and the seller makes money.

Arguments Against Organ Commerce

Critics of an organ market claim that the removal of a kidney presents an un- necessary risk to a "voluntary" donor. This concern would be especially relevant if the seller of a kidney were to end up with ESRD. The risks associated with the removal of a kidney, however, are comparable to the risks associated with com- mon bodily activities that are not illegal. These risks include occupations (for example, coal mining, fire fighting, and bomb rescue) and life-styles (for exam- ple, promiscuity, smoking, eating foods high in saturated fats, and drinking) that are arguably more risky than losing a kidney. Research has found that the risk to a healthy thirty-five-year-old of giving up a kidney is "equal to that incurred by driving a car 16 miles every working day." Therefore, if the removal of a kidney poses no more of a risk than accepted daily activities, the prohibition of organ commerce based on the "unnecessary risk" argument is unjustified. . . .

Another argument offered against financial inducements for organ donation contends that payment to donors will undermine and discourage acts of unpaid donation, and consequently erode the fibers of altruism in society. Proponents of commerce, however, posit that altruism can coexist with incentives. It does not necessarily follow that a person receiving incentives for a kidney has no al- truistic motives. An analogy can be drawn with tax deductible incentives on charitable donations: since the donor incurs a net loss even after the tax deduction, it is an act (at least partially) motivated by altruism. Similarly, then, an incentive may be a factor in the decision to donate a kidney, but the underlying motive may still be an altruistic concern. Also, supporters point out that "it may be incongruous and hypocritical that, when hospitals make volumes of money from transplantation, physicians and associated health professionals advance careers and incomes, drug companies profiteer, and the medical-industrial complex is enriched, the original donor of tissues is expected to be altruistic." By allowing commerce, donors are given an opportunity to use their resources to make money just as the other players do.

Exploiting the Poor?

Another concern about organ commerce is whether consent to donate a kidney is valid in cases of poverty. This argument suggests that monetary incentives are coercive and exploit the poor. The donor, however, has the ultimate power in the decision to give up a kidney. Although it may be a hard decision, it is not any more coercive than the accepted practice of living-related kidney donation. In such cases, some of the related donors suffer psychological and emotional pressure "(for example, perhaps by being the submissive and 'guilt'-ridden offspring of an extremely domineering and now ailing parent)." Then living-related donation should also be prohibited. Other acts that are induced by incentives

"Commerce in kidney transplantation . . . is consistent with current ethical standards in medicine."

should not be allowed either. For example, monetary incentives drive the demand for risky jobs such as ship-yard work, test piloting, and coal mining, and for athletics such as boxing and race car driving. Should these jobs be outlawed because there are incentives involved? Clearly, many Americans enjoy the benefits of the energy derived from coal in their homes; if this is the case, why not offer ESRD patients the convenience of a kidney transplant, and not having to dialyze for nine to twelve hours per week? Admittedly, this comparison is a bit far-fetched, but it illustrates the point that there are risky behaviors induced by incentives that are allowed in today's society. Further, the utilitarian argument is relevant in this discussion: the poor end up better off under a system of organ commerce because they reap substantial profits in the deal.

Building on the "exploitation" criticism, is there inherent inequality in allowing the sale of kidneys? Proponents of organ commerce point out that inequalities exist under current health policies (and these inequalities will continue because of future cost constraints). The wealthy are able to afford better insurance coverage and "better" doctors. Perhaps we abhor a market for kidneys because of the tension between our capitalist beliefs and egalitarian ideals. As Lester Carl Thurow pointed out, capitalism dictates that the wealthy are able to afford expensive treatments without considering medical effectiveness, and egalitarianism prohibits us from denying treatment to those who cannot afford medical care. I argue, however, that capitalism and egalitarianism can coexist under a system of organ commerce. When a person buys a kidney, the government is partially relieved of the high costs associated with dialysis. This long-term savings realized from the transplantation option can be used to finance a kidney purchasing program for the underprivileged. Indeed, a market for kidneys may serve to alleviate some inequities because the donor is well compensated.

There is also the universal criticism that commerce in organ transplantation results in the commodification of the body and instills a mind set of acquisitiveness in the young. Critics fail to recognize other acceptable forms of commodification. In the case of surrogate motherhood, women are paid for carrying a fetus to term. More widespread are instances of pornography. Just as women and men are given the freedom to express themselves in pornography, individuals deserve the right to do what they want with their bodies. Indeed, the latter argument closely parallels the right to abortion (even though the above examples are controversial, they are still legal under existing U.S. law). . . .

A Suggested Framework for Commerce in Donor Kidneys

The regulations listed below are in large part responses to worries about rampant commercialism. For each issue, I consider the advantages and pitfalls.

To alleviate the concern that there will be donors flown in from other countries, all parties should be citizens of the country in which the recipient resides. More specifically, it is the donor who should be able to prove his or her citizenship. Although this approach curtails the availability of kidneys, it is an important aspect for maintaining control. Other countries (especially third-world nations) tend to have fewer mechanisms to regulate markets. Take, for example, the new economic regime implemented in Russia—there have been numerous reports of unethical practices in the trade of goods (that is, black markets). Thus, instead of relying on an international supply of kidneys, the United States should utilize market mechanisms to increase the internal supply. (Although there is an inconsistency in forbidding cross-border sale of organs while permitting intramural commerce, pragmatic concerns dictate this policy.)

"Individuals should be allowed to do whatever they please with their bodies, including selling a kidney."

Independent teams of physicians should assess the condition of the donor's kidney in order to minimize the possibility of disease transmission (such as HIV and hepatitis). In fact, there should be a rigorous screening process to ensure the compatibility of the kidney with the patient, the quality of the kidney, and the safety of donation. A system of "informed consent" should be implemented. People deemed incompetent to understand the possible consequences of the procedure should not be allowed to participate. Along similar lines, a ninety-year-old man should not be allowed to sell a kidney. Thus, there should be a minimum and maximum age—the former to protect against exploiting juveniles, and the latter to avoid kidneys with limited function. How would this age bracket be set? Although any age is arbitrary, a minimum age of twenty-one and a maximum age of sixty would be reasonable in the beginning stages of this policy. After some controlled outcome studies, these ages could be adjusted to account for the quality of kidneys relative to age.

> *"Capitalism and egalitarianism can coexist under a system of organ commerce."*

In addition, all the parties involved in the transplantation procedure should charge the same fees as they normally do, regardless of the source of the kidney, including the physicians, drug companies, laboratories, and hospitals. Consistency in pricing would prevent the parties listed from selectively choosing more profitable cases.

The donor of the kidney should also be eligible for long-term health insurance. This policy would minimize the risk of any illness resulting from the transplantation procedure. The drawback of this approach is the large amount of money needed to insure all of the donors. Where would this money come from? I suggest that the recipients of the kidneys would pay into a government-run insurance scheme similar to Medicare. This coverage could be in the form of a lump-sum annuity at the time of donation or quarterly premiums similar to existing insurance schemes. Additional funds could be derived from the savings realized by the transplantation option. Taken together, a donor's long-term monetary commitment would help reduce the high costs associated with the government's ESRD program.

Preventing Abuse

As with other market goods, the trade of kidneys runs the risk of unethical practices such as blackmail and extortion. To combat rampant commercialization in organ commerce, however, there should be no brokers or private contractors allowed (any illegal transactions should be punished severely). Instead, a nonprofit government agency or voluntary organization (like the Red Cross) should be created and exclusively licensed to procure and coordinate the transfer of a kidney. In addition to matching the donor with a patient, the agency should periodically review and publish the results of the program to keep the public informed.

Taken together, a grossly simplified scenario is as follows: Jack suffers from ESRD and needs a kidney. He cannot find a relative willing to donate a kidney so he goes to the Department of Organ Sharing (DOS). Jill, a healthy thirty-two-year-old, goes to DOS and is willing to donate a kidney for the going amount of $50,000. After a rigorous psychiatric and physical examination by an independent team of doctors, Jill is found to be an appropriate candidate for donation. She signs an "informed consent" form detailing her rights, and heads for the hospital. After the transplantation procedure, Jack continues to pay into a fund to provide for Jill's government-run insurance. Indeed, Jack and Jill both benefit from the transaction.

The case for commerce in organ transplantation holds if the advantages of a market approach are recognized. These advantages include: (1) the libertarian notion of protecting autonomy; (2) the utilitarian assertion of maximizing happiness—since the transaction involves willing agents, both the buyer and seller are better off; (3) financial incentives increasing the supply of transplantable kidneys. . . .

> *"In a recent study, it was found that the majority of the general public favored the sale of a kidney as long as there was strict regulation of the practice."*

A framework for the sale of kidneys would be as follows: (1) All parties would have to be U.S. citizens. (2) A rigorous screening process would analyze the physical and mental health of the donor, age, and risk of disease transmission. (3) The donor and recipient would both have independent teams of physicians. (4) Long-term health care would be made available to the donor by a government-run program. (5) No brokers or private contractors would be allowed. (6) A nonprofit government agency or voluntary organization would oversee the transfer of the kidney.

The final point I would like to make is that public and professional opinion will decide this issue in the future. In a recent study, it was found that the majority of the general public favored the sale of a kidney as long as there was strict regulation of the practice. Therefore, with enough public and professional support, commerce in organ transplantation may become a viable mechanism to contain the future costs of treating ESRD patients.

Commerce in Organs Is Unethical

by Stephen G. Post

About the author: *Stephen G. Post is a professor at the Center for Biomedical Ethics at Case Western Reserve University and the author of* Inquiries in Bioethics.

Should we allow competent adults to sell their organs and tissues? The libertarian view, with its doctrine that freedom is the highest value, constrained only by the prohibition against harm to others (the "harm principle") but not to self, would allow the sale of body parts. Even on this view, proponents stop short of condoning the sale of vital organs, for this would result in death, although the logic of libertarianism would seem to allow even this. Libertarians would not be justifying the potential sale of spare body parts if there were no demand. As biomedical science advances in areas such as reproductive technology, fetal tissue transplant and organ transplantation, market incentives appear to be one way in which supply might meet escalating demands.

A Market for Fetal Tissue?

There has been resistance to the commercialization of body parts. For example, the National Institutes of Health now funds research in fetal transplants for Parkinson's disease patients. The NIH is clear, however, that no pregnant woman can sell her fetus. NIH ethics guidelines assume that if financial incentives were allowed, poor women surely would become pregnant in order to make money through aborting the fetus, optimally at the beginning of the second trimester when the fetus has developed sufficiently but still contains undifferentiated brain cells, and selling the fetus to physicians or to patients with neurodegenerative diseases.

The utility of fetal tissue transplant still is debated, particularly in light of other possible medical therapies under development. But imagine what could happen if fetal tissue transplants were to work effectively as a cure or partial cure for the diseases of Alzheimer's and diabetes. The demand quickly would reach into the tens of millions. Four million people in the United States have Alzheimer's disease, and the number will triple as the baby boomers become elderly. For the Parkinson's operation, at least three to four fetuses are needed per transplant (a dime-size hole is drilled into the top of the skull, and fetal brain cells are implanted on the outer brain surface.) The libertarian proclaims "long live freedom," and in the meantime, the problems of poverty and of children having children are finally solved—a welfare conservative's dream. Caregivers for people with various dementing diseases might be liberated from a sea of diapers and nursing home payments.

A Form of Oppression

The critics of commercialization of the fetus quickly point to the injustice of it all: The poor become pregnant to earn money that ultimately comes from the wealthier classes. Surely a wealthy woman who is financially comfortable will not need to sell fetuses. A poor woman might be able to sell four fetuses a year, perhaps at several thousand dollars each. Perhaps the moral ambiguity of abortion will entirely disappear in a culture that establishes a new profession in fetal sales. While this is all rather futuristic, it should be remembered that in India, where a huge black market in nonvital body parts provides kidneys for the wealthy, it is the poor who sell. Is this truly freedom, as the libertarian proclaims? Or is it a forced choice made in destitution and contrary to the seller's true human nature? I see such a market as the most demeaning form of human oppression, as unworthy of any valid human freedom, and as reducing the unborn child to mere grist in the medical mill.

"In addition to the risk of creating a class of oppressed sellers . . . there is a second specter associated with the market approach: low-quality parts."

The NIH rightly forbids the sale of fetuses, as well as the designation of particular fetal-tissue recipients such as a father or some other loved one, for fear of emotional pressure on the donor. Of course, even on the current basis of voluntary donation, many are disturbed by the very idea of encouraging the "harvesting" of fetuses as an act of beneficence, akin to donating blood. Will signs on buses read, "Be a giver of life. Donate your fetus today"?

Writing in 1971, Richard Titmuss lamented the commercialization of the blood supply in the United States. He wrote that "proportionately more blood is being supplied by the poor, the unskilled, the unemployed, Negroes and other low-income groups." He warned of a new class of exploited "high blood yielders" and of redistribution of blood from poor to rich. Fortunately, by 1982 only 3 to 4 percent of blood came from paid donors. Moreover, various social scientific studies indicated that the American people favored a voluntary system and were disturbed by the buying and selling of blood. Personal solicitation, coupled with more convenient donation opportunities, had proved to be highly effective.

In addition to the risk of creating a class of oppressed sellers (who might provide organs, bone marrow, blood and ova, in addition to fetuses), there is a second specter associated with the market approach: low-quality parts. Titmuss warned against the increasing danger to the American blood supply due to contagion. The sale of blood is forbidden by the American Red Cross because sales two decades ago included samples of blood from people infected with pathogens. Drug addicts, for example, routinely sold blood, thereby passing on diseases such as hepatitis. Because those who sell are inevitably the most needy and marginalized, the likelihood of contagion is great. The blood supply is now much purer because it relies entirely on volunteerism. Sperm is sold and must be carefully tested for contagion. Still, a small number of women have become HIV infected as a result of receiving tainted sperm. Spare parts, tissues and body fluids gathered for a fee are, on the whole, of poor quality.

> *"A sacred dimension to the body places limits on our human authority to 'own' it."*

Oppression of the poor and poor quality are concerns that fall under the moral rubric of "do no harm." There is another concern that involves not the avoidance of harm but the doing of good. When the call goes out to a community for bone marrow, blood or some other lifesaving bodily substance, the spirit of beneficence is tapped. Often, we discover within ourselves a moral idealism that serves the neighbor in the form of disinterested love. In an age of considerable greed and solipsism, the expression of connectedness with unknown others is a welcome sight. Volunteerism allows the community to express moral idealism when moral minimalism is the order of the day. The marketing of body parts undercuts and even eradicates one of the important implementations of the philanthropic conscience.

Last fall this point was driven home to millions of Italians—their country has one of the world's lowest donation rates—by the selfless example of two American tourists. During a foiled robbery attempt, Italian bandits had killed the 7-year-old son of Reginald and Maggie Green of Bodega Bay, Calif. The decision by the couple to donate their son's organs stunned the nation as a gesture of extraordinary generosity and triggered an outpouring of organ donations.

The Body Is Not Merely Property

Finally, there is the issue of human dignity and the body as property. In most religious traditions the body has not been perceived as a possession over which one has property rights. Instead, it has been interpreted as that over which we have stewardship. In general terms, human beings are responsible for their bodies as stewards or caretakers, but they do not own their bodies, which are ultimately the property of the creator. Hence, the classical argument against suicide in Western culture was always, "God giveth life, and God taketh away." The ultimate authority over the body and over bodily life is God, and that ought not to be usurped. In the most general terms, then, a sacred dimension to the body places limits on our human authority to "own" it. For this reason, Jewish, Roman Catholic and Protestant ethics emphasized the integrity of the body, the sin of self-mutilation and respectful treatment of the body even after death. Hence, when the first cornea transplants emerged, theologians seriously debated whether cornea procurement violates "integrity."

Despite the success of transplantation during the last three decades, there are too few who donate body parts. This is largely because on some deep psychological level, human beings are reluctant to have themselves or their loved ones "picked apart." Medical anthropologists have long observed that Asian Pan-Confucianism, from China to Japan, forbids donating body parts because the body is bequeathed by one's ancestors, so that to mutilate it is to violate filial duties. Orthodox Judaism categorically condemns organ procurement from the living and the dead. On one hand, these traditions can be dismissed as archaic, to be set aside by rational, empirical, scientific progress. It appears, however, that they articulate a universal anxiety about taking such liberties with the body.

> *"When blood procurement relied on selling, there was considerably less blood available than there is now."*

Enter here the libertarians. If spare parts are scarce, if no degree of appeal to beneficence seems to dramatically elevate the levels of procurement, then why not move past archaic anxieties by enlisting the almighty dollar? After all, people will do just about anything for money, even if they feel that they violate the body's moral demand for respect.

Commercialism Undermines Community

To some degree, we have succeeded in negotiating with tradition by creating a culture of giving and receiving body parts. True, there are organ shortages, but procurement is steady. To go from the reasonably successful moral idealism of generous giving and grateful receiving to selling and buying certainly undermines the spirit of community. Moreover, selling and buying may not even produce the desired results in increased supply. When blood procurement relied on selling, there was considerably less blood available than there is now. We have taken on highly symbolic meanings. Commercialization may repulse rather than entice.

True, commercialization has begun to emerge. Sperm, eggs and surrogate wombs are sold and bought. In India, the sale of a kidney ensures comfort for one's family. Before it is too late, I recommend a categorical ban on all sales of body parts in the U.S., and a renewed appeal to the philanthropic conscience that lies within us all, even if obscured by the ubiquity of the profit motive.

Commerce in Organs Could Save Lives

by Pete du Pont

About the author: *Pete du Pont is the former governor of Delaware and policy chairman of the National Center for Policy Analysis.*

There are currently about 45,000 people waiting for a human-organ transplant. About 3,000 of them will die on that waiting list because a suitable transplant organ will not become available in time. The short supply of organs has recently led to some overt attempts to ration them in a way that would be more beneficial to society.

Rationing Organs

For example, the United Network for Organ Sharing (UNOS) has altered its guidelines for those needing a liver transplant so that those with acute liver problems get priority. Those with a chronic liver condition like hepatitis or cirrhosis (which could be the result of alcohol abuse) cannot rise above the second level in priority status.

In addition, the legislature in the state of Washington recently passed legislation—which the governor vetoed for being too vague—that would prohibit those on Death Row from receiving "lifesaving health care procedures" such as an organ transplant. Now the Cleveland Clinic is being accused of removing organs before some patients are legally dead.

Instead of looking for new ways to ration organs or take them prematurely, we should ask how we can increase the supply of organs so that doctors are not forced to decide who lives and who dies. The answer is to compensate donors for their organs. Unfortunately, doing so is currently against the law. That's because the National Organ Transplant Act (1984) prohibits "any person to knowingly acquire, receive or otherwise transfer any human organ for valuable consideration for use in human transplantation."

As a result, altruism is the only legal motive for individuals or their surrogates to donate their organs. But while altruism is a noble motive, it is seldom a

Reprinted from Pete du Pont, "Have a Heart—but Pay Me for It," *San Diego Union-Tribune*, September 29, 1997, with permission from the author.

compelling one. Economic theory clearly recognizes that when demand for a good or service is high, its price will increase until the supply and demand reach an equilibrium. If the price is prohibited from rising, a shortage will occur because people will not provide a product when the price is too low.

Thus, permitting donors to receive some type of compensation for their organs would help alleviate our organ-shortage problem. Opponents of a market for organs immediately conjure up images of strange people selling off body parts. But a market for organs could develop in a number of ways: Some would be more open and direct, while others might be indirect and incorporate the concerns of some of those who oppose compensation.

Several Approaches to Compensation

We could, for example:

• Permit a donor pool. Dr. Robert M. Sade, a surgeon and professor of medicine at the Medical University of South Carolina, and his colleagues have proposed to create an in-kind market for organs. Every adult would be given the option of joining the Transplant Recipient and Donor Organization (TRADO). Membership would require permission to have your organs removed at death, and only those joining would be permitted to receive a transplanted organ.

Those who chose not to join would be electing for standard medical care, short of transplantation. Thus, the only way to receive an organ while living would be to have given permission to have your organs taken at death.

• Permit people to receive after-death compensation. A person wanting to become an organ donor would simply contract with an organ-donor organization, which would compensate the deceased's estate for each organ successfully harvested. The compensation could be in a variety of forms. A hospital or organ-donor network might pay part or all of a donor's burial expenses, for example.

Such a provision might encourage lower-income people who could not afford life insurance to sign up for the program as a way to provide for their funeral costs. (A similar provision has been supported by an article in the *Journal of the American Medical Association*.)

• Contribute funds to the donor's designated charity—a hospital, university, or social services agency. Let people sell whatever they want, when they want. The most open and market-oriented approach would be to let anyone who wanted to sell one or

> *"Permitting donors to receive some type of compensation for their organs would help alleviate our organ-shortage problem."*

more organs do so. Thus, if someone needed a kidney and was willing to pay for one, a compatible donor could provide the recipient with a kidney for the market-set price.

A variation on this proposal would let people sell their organs now at a discounted price for harvesting after death. There are obvious dangers in this approach that would need more thought before it is adopted. The pressures on people unable to make knowledgeable decisions might be prohibitive.

A Market for Organs Would Save Lives

The point is, there are ways to encourage people to donate their organs to help others live. These mechanisms would increase the supply of organs, the waiting lines and needless deaths would decrease if not disappear, and donors and recipients would have more choices. While opponents to these proposals want more organs, they don't want a market for organs. Paternalistically, they impose their values on everyone else. And with regard to organ availability, while paternalism lives, people die.

Commerce in Organs Has Led to Human Rights Violations

by David J. Rothman

About the author: *David J. Rothman is a professor of social medicine at the Columbia College of Physicians and Surgeons and the author of several books, including* Medicine and Western Civilization.

[Since the mid-1980s,] transplanting human organs has become a standard and remarkably successful medical procedure, giving new life to thousands of people with failing hearts, kidneys, livers, and lungs. But very few countries have sufficient organs to meet patients' needs. In the United States, for example, some 50,000 people are on the waiting list for a transplant; fifteen percent of patients who need a new heart will die before one becomes available. The shortages are even more acute throughout the Middle East and Asia.

Desperation and Greed

This lack of available organs arouses desperation and rewards greed. Would-be recipients are willing to travel far to get an organ and many surgeons, brokers, and government officials will do nearly anything to profit from the shortage. In India well-to-do people and their doctors buy kidneys from debt-ridden Indian villagers; in China officials profitably market organs of executed Chinese prisoners. The international commerce in organs is unregulated, indeed anarchic. We know a good deal about trafficking in women and children for sex. We are just beginning to learn about the trafficking in organs for transplantation.

The routes that would-be organ recipients follow are well known to both doctors and patients. Italians (who have the lowest rate of organ donation in Europe) travel to Belgium to obtain their transplants; so do Israelis, who lately have also been going to rural Turkey and bringing their surgeons along with them. Residents of the Gulf States, Egyptians, Malaysians, and Bangladeshis mainly go to India for organs. In the Pacific, Koreans, Japanese, and Taiwanese, along with the residents of Hong Kong and Singapore, fly to China. Less frequently, South Americans go to Cuba and citizens of the former Soviet Union go to Russia. Americans for the most part stay home, but well-to-do foreigners come to the United States for transplants, and some centers allot up to 10 percent of their organs to them.

The Rapid Spread of Transplantation Techniques

All of these people are responding to the shortages of organs that followed on the discovery of cyclosporine in the early 1980s. Until then, transplantation had been a risky and experimental procedure, typically a last-ditch effort to stave off death; the problem was not the complexity of the surgery but the body's immune system, which attacked and rejected the new organ as though it were a foreign object. Cyclosporine moderated the response while not suppressing the immune system's reactions to truly infectious agents. As a result, in countries with sophisticated medical programs, kidney and heart transplantation became widely used and highly successful procedures. Over 70 percent of heart transplant recipients were living four years later. Ninety-two percent of patients who received a kidney from a living donor were using that kidney one year later; 81 percent of the cases were doing so four years later, and in 40 to 50 percent of the cases, ten years later.

> *"This lack of available organs arouses desperation and rewards greed."*

Transplantation spread quickly from developed to less developed countries. By 1990, kidneys were being transplanted in nine Middle Eastern, six South American, two North African, and two sub-Saharan African countries. Kidney transplants are by far the most common, since kidney donors can live normal lives with one kidney, while kidneys are subject to disease from a variety of causes, including persistent high blood pressure, adult diabetes, nephritis (inflammation of vessels that filter blood), and infections, which are more usually found in poor countries. (It is true that the donor runs the risk that his remaining kidney will become diseased, but in developed countries, at least, this risk is small.) The transplant techniques, moreover, are relatively simple. Replacing one heart with another, for example, is made easier by the fact that the blood-carrying vessels that must be detached from the one organ and reattached to the other are large and relatively easy to handle. (A transplant surgeon told me that if you can tie your shoes, you can transplant a heart.) . . .

Reluctance to Donate

With patient demand for transplantation so strong and the medical capacity to satisfy it so widespread, shortages of organs were bound to occur. Most of the doctors and others involved in early transplants expected that organs would be readily donated as a gift of life from the dead, an exchange that cost the donor nothing and brought the recipient obvious benefits. However, it turns out that powerful cultural and religious taboos discourage donation, not only in countries with strong religious establishments but in more secular ones as well. The issue has recently attracted the attention of anthropologists, theologians, and literary scholars, and some of their findings are brought together in the fascinating collection of essays, *Organ Transplantation: Meanings and Realities*. . . .

> *"Americans say they favor transplantation but turn out to be very reluctant to donate organs."*

Americans say they favor transplantation but turn out to be very reluctant to donate organs. Despite countless public education campaigns, organ donation checkoffs on drivers' licenses, and laws requiring health professionals to ask families to donate the organs of a deceased relative, the rates of donation have not risen during the past five years and are wholly inadequate to the need. As of May 1997, according to the United Network for Organ Sharing, 36,000 people were awaiting a kidney transplant, 8,000 a liver transplant, and 3,800 a heart transplant. One recent study found that when families were asked by hospitals for permission to take an organ from a deceased relative, 53 percent flatly refused. . . .

If organs are in such short supply, how do some countries manage to fill the needs of foreigners? The answers vary. Belgium has a surplus of organs because it relies upon a "presumed consent" statute that probably would be rejected in every American state. Under its provisions, you must formally register your unwillingness to serve as a donor; otherwise, upon your death, physicians are free to transplant your organs. To object you must go to the town hall, make your preference known, and have your name registered on a national computer roster; when a death occurs, the hospital checks the computer base, and unless your name appears on it, surgeons may use your organs, notwithstanding your family's objections. . . .

Because its system of presumed consent has worked so well, Belgium has a surplus of organs and will provide them to foreigners. However, it will not export them, say, to Milan or Tel Aviv, which would be entirely feasible. Instead, it requires that patients in need of a transplant come to Belgium, which then benefits from the surgical fees paid to doctors and hospitals.

The Market for Human Organs in India

Not surprisingly, money counts even more in India, which has an abundant supply of kidneys because physicians and brokers bring together the desperately poor with the desperately ill. The sellers include impoverished villagers, slum dwellers, power-loom operators, manual laborers, and daughters-in-law with small dowries. The buyers come from Egypt, Kuwait, Oman, and other Gulf States, and from India's enormous middle class (which numbers at least

200 million). They readily pay between $2,500 and $4,000 for a kidney (of which the donor, if he is not cheated, will receive between $1,000 and $1,500) and perhaps two times that for the surgery. From the perspective of patients with end-stage renal disease, there is no other choice. For largely cultural reasons, hardly any organs are available from cadavers; dialysis centers are scarce and often a source of infection, and only a few people are able to administer dialysis to themselves at home (as is also the case in the US). Thus it is not surprising that a flourishing transplant business has emerged in such cities as Bangalore, Bombay, and Madras.

The market in organs has its defenders. To refuse the sellers a chance to make the money they need, it is said, would be an unjustifiable form of paternalism. Moreover, the sellers may not be at greater risk living with one kidney, at least according to US research. A University of Minnesota transplant team compared seventy-eight kidney donors with their siblings twenty years or more after the surgery took place, and found no significant differences between them in health; indeed, risk-conscious insurance companies do not raise their rates for kidney donors. And why ban the sale of kidneys when the sale of other body parts, including semen, female eggs, hair, and blood, is allowed in many countries? The argument that these are renewable body parts is not persuasive if life without a kidney does not compromise health. Finally, transplant surgeons, nurses, and social workers, as well as transplant retrieval teams and the hospitals, are all paid for their work. Why should only the donor and the donor's family go without compensation?

A Degrading Practice

But because some body parts have already been turned into commodities does not mean that an increasing trade in kidneys and other organs is desirable. To poor Indians, as Margaret Radin, professor of law at Stanford, observes, "Commodification worries may seem like a luxury. Yet, taking a slightly longer view, commodification threatens the personhood of everyone, not just those who can now afford to concern themselves about it." Many of the poor Indians who sell their organs clearly feel they have had to submit to a degrading practice in order to get badly needed sums of money. They would rather not have parts of their body cut out, an unpleasant experience at best, and one that is probably more risky in Bombay than in Minnesota. Radin concludes: "Desperation is the social problem that we should be looking at, rather than the market ban. . . .We must rethink the larger social context in which this dilemma is embedded.". . .

"Because some body parts have already been turned into commodities does not mean that an increasing trade in kidneys and other organs is desirable."

China is at the center of the Pacific routes to organ transplantation because it has adopted the tactic of harvesting the organs of executed prisoners. In 1984, immediately after cyclosporine became available, the government issued a document entitled "Rules Concerning the Utilization of Corpses or Organs from the Corpses of Executed Prisoners." Kept confidential, the new law provided that organs from executed prisoners could be used for transplants if the prisoner agreed, if the family agreed, or if no one came to claim the body. (Robin Munro of Human Rights Watch/Asia brought the law to light.) That the law lacks an ethical basis according to China's own values is apparent from its stipulations. "The use of corpses or organs of executed prisoners must be kept strictly secret," it stated, "and attention must be paid to avoiding negative repercussions." The cars used to retrieve organs from the execution grounds cannot bear health department insignia; the people involved in obtaining organs are not permitted to wear white uniforms. In my own interviews with Chinese transplant surgeons, none would admit to the practice; when I showed them copies of the law, they shrugged and said it was news to them.

> *"Many of the poor Indians who sell their organs clearly feel they have had to submit to a degrading practice in order to get badly needed sums of money."*

But not to other Asian doctors. Physicians in Japan, Hong Kong, Singapore, and Taiwan, among other countries, serve as travel agents, directing their patients to hospitals in Wuhan, Beijing, and Shanghai. The system is relatively efficient. Foreigners do not have to wait days or weeks for an organ to be made available; executions can be timed to meet market needs and the supply is more than adequate. China keeps the exact number of executions secret but Amnesty International calculates on the basis of executions reported in newspapers that there are at least 4,500 a year, and perhaps three to four times as many. Several years ago a heart transplant surgeon told me that he had just been invited to China to perform a transplant; accustomed to long waiting periods in America, he asked how he could be certain that a heart would be available when he arrived. His would-be hosts told him they would schedule an execution to fit with his travel schedule. He turned down the invitation. In February 1998 the FBI arrested two Chinese nationals living in New York for allegedly soliciting payment for organs from executed prisoners to be transplanted in China.

An Obvious Violation of Medical Ethics

China's system also has its defenders. Why waste the organs? Why deprive prisoners of the opportunity to do a final act of goodness? But once again, the objections should be obvious. The idea that prisoners on death row—which in China is a miserable hovel in a local jail—can give informed consent to their donations is absurd. Moreover, there is no way of ensuring that the need for organs might not influence courtroom verdicts. A defendant's guilt may be unclear, but if he has a long criminal record, why not condemn him so that a worthy citizen might live?

To have physicians retrieve human organs at an execution, moreover, subverts the ethical integrity of the medical profession. There are almost no reliable eyewitness accounts of Chinese practices, but until 1994, Taiwan also authorized transplants of organs from executed prisoners, and its procedures are probably duplicated in China. Immediately before the execution, the physician sedates the prisoner and then inserts both a breathing tube in his lungs and a catheter in one of his veins. The prisoner is then executed with a bullet to his head; the physician immediately moves to stem the blood flow, attach a respirator to the breathing tube, and inject drugs into the catheter so as to increase blood pressure and cardiac output. With the organs thus maintained, the body is transported to a hospital where the donor is waiting and the surgery is performed. The physicians have become intimate participants in the executions; instead of protecting life, they are manipulating the consequences of death.

The motive for all such practices is money. The Europeans, Middle Easterners, and Asians who travel to China, India, Belgium, and other countries pay handsomely for their new organs and in hard currencies. Depending on the organization of the particular health care system and the level of corruption, their fees will enrich surgeons or medical centers, or both. Many of the surgeons I interviewed were quite frank about how important the income from transplants was to their hospitals, but they were far more reluctant to say how much of it they kept for themselves. Still, a leading transplant surgeon in Russia is well known for his vast estate and passion for horses. His peers in India and China may be less ostentatious but not necessarily less rich. They will all claim to be doing good, rescuing patients from near death. . . .

> *"China . . . has adopted the tactic of harvesting the organs of executed prisoners."*

Physicians Must Oppose the Sale of Organs

Almost all major national and international medical bodies have opposed the sale of organs and the transplantation of organs from executed prisoners; but none of the medical organizations has been willing to take action to enforce their views. The World Medical Association in 1984, 1987, and 1994 condemned "the purchase and sale of human organs for transplantation." But it asks "governments of all countries to take effective steps," and has adopted no measures of its own. It has also criticized the practice of using organs from executed prisoners without their consent; but it fails to ask whether consent on death row can be meaningful. The association leaves it to national medical societies to "severely discipline the physicians involved." Neither it nor any other medical organization has imposed sanctions on violators.

The Bellagio Task Force [an international group including transplant surgeons, human rights activists, and social scientists] has posed several challenges to the international medical societies. What would happen if they took their proclaimed principles seriously, established a permanent monitoring body, and kept close surveillance on organ donation practices? What if they threatened to withhold training fellowships from countries which tolerated exploitative practices? What if they refused to hold international meetings in those countries, and, as was the case with South Africa under apartheid, did not allow physicians

> *"To have physicians retrieve human organs at an execution . . . subverts the ethical integrity of the medical profession."*

from those countries to attend their meetings? Why, moreover, couldn't the Novartis company, the manufacturer of cyclosporine, insist that it would sell its product only to doctors and hospitals that meet strict standards in obtaining organs? Such measures would be likely to have a serious effect, certainly in India, probably even in China. But as with the organs themselves, the willingness of doctors to use the moral authority of medicine as a force for change has, so far, been in short supply.

Chapter 3

Are Reproductive
Technologies Ethical?

Reproductive Technologies: An Overview

by Karen Wright

About the author: *Karen Wright is a contributor to* Discover *magazine.*

"Mommy, where do babies come from?" Parents have dreaded this question ever since the stork made its first delivery. But today's mommies and daddies have more explaining to do than their own parents could possibly have imagined. Though the birds and bees discussion was never easy, its elements were fairly straightforward: the fireworks exploding, the train chugging through the tunnel, the waves pounding the shore, the occasional reference to anatomy. Once upon a time, baby-making was synonymous with whoopee-making, and frozen eggs were for pastry dough, and seven was how many times you should let the phone ring before you hang up, not how many fetuses you could fit in a womb.

The Wild West of Medicine

These days, though, the facts of life can sound a lot like science fiction, as late-twentieth-century humanity grapples with the rise of noncoital conception. There are now more than a dozen ways to make a baby, the vast majority of which bypass the antiquated act of sexual congress. The last three decades have seen the advent of such high-tech interventions as fertility drugs, in vitro fertilization, donor eggs, donor sperm, donor embryos, and surrogate mothering. In the works are still more advanced technologies, such as the transfer of cell nuclei, embryo splitting, and even, if at least one man has his way, the cloning of human adults.

These techniques generally are gathered under the heading of "assisted reproduction." All the ones in use today were pioneered for and are usually employed by infertile couples of childbearing age. But they are also used by people with less conventional notions of parenting—singles, postmenopausal women, and gay partners. In the near future, assisted reproduction may become standard procedure for anyone who wants to conceive, and who can afford it. The allure, of course, is control: control over the timing of parenthood, control over "embryo quality," control over genetic disease, control over less pernicious characteristics, such as gender, that are also determined by genes.

So far, owing to federal policy and societal preference, the practice of assisted reproduction is largely unregulated. One specialist has even called it the Wild West of medicine. It's also expensive, bothersome, inefficient, and fraught with ethical complications—but none of those considerations has slowed its growth. Since 1978, when the first test-tube baby was born, the

> *"In the near future, assisted reproduction may become standard procedure for anyone who wants to conceive, and who can afford it."*

number of fertility clinics in the United States has gone from less than 30 to more than 300. The multibillion-dollar fertility industry has created tens of thousands of babies. Assisted reproduction has relieved the anguish of men and women who, just decades ago, would have had to abandon their hopes of having children. It's also created a world where a dead man can impregnate a stranger, where a woman can rent out her uterus, and where a child can have five parents—and still end up an orphan. It's not at all clear how this new world will change the meaning of family. But it has already transformed what used to be known as the miracle of birth.

Fertility Drugs

In November 1997 in Iowa a couple made history, national television, and the covers of *Time* and *Newsweek* when their seven babies were born alive. "We're trusting in God," the McCaugheys told reporters when asked how they would cope with the sudden surfeit of offspring. But to conceive for the second time, Bobbi McCaughey had trusted in Metrodin, a fertility drug that stimulates the ripening of eggs in the ovaries. A woman on Metrodin can produce dozens of eggs in a month instead of just one.

Metrodin belongs to a suite of hormones that are used to increase egg development and release, or ovulation. Fertility drugs go by many brand names, like Clomid, Pergonal, Humegon, Fertinex, Follistim, and some have been around for decades. Women who have problems ovulating regularly can often conceive by the time-honored method once fertility drugs have improved their chances of success.

Even so, taking fertility drugs is not like taking aspirin. Most are administered by daily injections that couples are trained to perform. The drugs themselves aren't cheap—a single dose of Fertinex, for example, is about $60—and most doctors monitor the progress of egg ripening with ultrasound scans and blood tests that add to the overall cost. Ultimately, a cycle of treatment with fertility drugs may cost more than $1,500.

And there are risks. The most common is multiple pregnancy: the simultaneous conception of two or (many) more fetuses, like the McCaugheys'. Despite the celebratory atmosphere that greeted the Iowa septuplets, such pregnancies are in fact a grave predicament for would-be parents. Multiple pregnancies increase the odds of maternal complications such as high blood pressure and diabetes. And they pose even greater risks for the unborn. The fetuses gestating in a multiple pregnancy are far more susceptible than their singlet peers to miscarriage, birth defects, low birth weight, and premature birth, as well as lifelong problems that can result from prematurity—including cerebral palsy, blindness, kidney failure, and mental retardation.

There are ways to get around the problem of multiple pregnancy. One is to abstain from sex if ultrasound scans reveal that a plethora of eggs is poised for release. Statistics suggest, however, that many couples choose not to exercise this option. Whereas in the general population the rate of multiple pregnancy is 1 to 2 percent, the rate among women treated with fertility drugs can be as high as 25 percent.

Another way to deal with the risks of multiple pregnancy is to eliminate some fetuses before they are born. Infertility specialists call this technique selective reduction. It is performed before the third month of pregnancy by injecting selected fetuses with potassium chloride, which stops the heart. A doctor inserts a needle through the abdomen or vagina of the mother-to-be to deliver the injection.

> *"Like most techniques of assisted reproduction, selective reduction introduces ethical problems as it solves medical ones."*

Like most techniques of assisted reproduction, selective reduction introduces ethical problems as it solves medical ones. For many couples, the decision of whether and how much to reduce is traumatic. Some, including the McCaugheys, simply refuse to do it. Others accept the agony—and irony—of destroying surplus fetuses as an unfortunate consequence of their condition. Yet still other people feel comfortable enough with the technique to use it for practical, rather than medical, reasons. "There are patients that will push very hard to reduce from three fetuses to two," says Benjamin Younger, executive director of the American Society for Reproductive Medicine. "They'll say, 'Doctor, I can't cope with triplets.'". . .

In Vitro Fertilization

Kathryn Graven and her husband decided to start a family when Graven was 34. After nine months of trying by the usual route, they went to an area clinic for a fertility workup. There are various causes of infertility, including hormonal imbalance in women, low sperm count in men, and blockages in the reproductive tract of either partner. But tests failed to identify a specific cause for the Gravens', so their doctor recommended conservative treatment. In each of three months, Graven tried the fertility drug Clomid, which is taken orally, to stimulate egg production, followed by artificial insemination with her husband's sperm. When that didn't work, Graven switched to Fertinex, which is injected beneath the skin. After two rounds of Fertinex and artificial insemination also failed, the couple decided to try in vitro fertilization.

In vitro fertilization (IVF) is the cornerstone of assisted reproductive technology. The procedure—in which ripe eggs are removed from the ovaries and incubated with sperm—greatly improves the haphazard gambit of traditional in vivo fertilization. It also introduces another level of complexity and expense. In addition to egg-ripening hormones, a woman undergoing IVF will usually take a protean cocktail of drugs designed to suppress and then trigger the release of mature eggs. Egg retrieval, done by guiding a hollow needle through the wall of the vagina and into the nearby ovaries, is characterized as a minor surgical procedure. ("The next day I felt like a Roto-Rooter had gone through my insides," says Graven.) And then the fertilized embryos have to be transferred back to the uterus.

When Graven's IVF attempt failed as well, her doctor recommended a more advanced technique: gamete intrafallopian transfer, or GIFT. In this procedure, eggs are harvested, mixed with sperm, then returned to the fallopian tubes—where egg and sperm normally meet—to fertilize. GIFT requires a longer and more complicated operation, with three incisions in the patient's abdomen, and about two days' recovery. But the success rates are 5 to 10 percent higher than those of IVF. It worked for Graven: she is due to give birth in July [1998], at the age of 37.

Low Rates of Success

GIFT is one of several variations on the IVF theme that were introduced in the 1980s as infertility specialists sought to expand their skills in assisted reproduction. Even with these innovations, however, the efficacy of assisted reproduction is sobering. Graven's experience was typical of what many infertile couples might undergo, except in one respect: Graven got pregnant. Success rates for IVF depend on a patient's age and vary from clinic to clinic and from procedure to procedure. But the ballpark figure—the so-called take-home baby rate—is one live birth for every five IVF cycles. Infertility specialists point out that the success rates for these procedures increase every year and that in any given month a fertile couple's chance of conceiving by traditional means is also one in five. According to the American Society for Reproductive Medicine, more than half of all infertile couples could attain pregnancy if they persisted long enough with treatments for assisted reproduction.

> *"In vitro fertilization (IVF) is the cornerstone of assisted reproductive technology."*

But that also means that about half will never have a baby, no matter how much therapy they get. And one thing about making babies by the usual means is that it's free. If at first you don't succeed, you can try, try again, without taking out a second mortgage. A single cycle of IVF, on the other hand, costs between $8,000 and $10,000. Special options like GIFT may cost more. Graven didn't have to pay for most of her treatment, because Massachusetts is one of ten states that mandate insurance coverage for infertility treatment. The bill for her pregnancy would have been well over $25,000.

> *"Assisted reproduction also invites the preselection of embryos based on genetic traits, and all the moral dilemmas that may accrue thereto."*

Is it worth it? The market says yes. Although rates of infertility have remained constant, demand for infertility services has risen steadily in the past two decades. Today about 6 million couples in the United States have fertility problems; half of them go to their doctors for help, and about a quarter end up trying assisted reproduction. Whether those couples view these attempts as a blessing or a curse "depends on the outcome," says Margaret Hollister, director of the help line at Resolve, a national infertility support group based in Somerville, Massachusetts. "The treatments are stressful, expensive, and require a big time commitment.". . .

Ethical Dilemmas Abound

Moreover, pursuing parenthood via assisted reproduction means being confronted with ethical decisions well outside the range of most people's moral radars. Because IVF techniques often give rise to multiple pregnancies, selective reduction is an issue here as well. Couples undergoing IVF must also decide how many eggs to fertilize and transfer at one time (which bears on the question of multiple pregnancy), whether they want to create and freeze embryos for future use, and what the eventual disposition of any unused frozen embryos should be. Former spouses have waged custody battles over frozen embryos, and in at least one case the attending IVF clinic claimed the embryo as its lawful property. Legally, human embryos occupy a gray area all their own, somewhere between human life and some rarefied form of property.

Assisted reproduction also invites the preselection of embryos based on genetic traits, and all the moral dilemmas that may accrue thereto. Screening is done by removing a single cell from an eight-cell embryo and analyzing the chromosomes or DNA in the cell nucleus. Already some clinics offer to screen in vitro embryos for genes related to cystic fibrosis, hemophilia, and muscular dystrophy. Couples can decide which of the embryos they've created meet their specifications; the rejected embryos can be discarded or donated to research.

Finally, assisted reproduction has opened the door to all manner of gamete swapping and surrogacy, from the simplest and oldest method—artificial insemination with a donor's sperm—to more complex scenarios in which any combination of donor eggs, donor sperm, and donor embryos may be used. In addition to biological surrogate motherhood (the method that created the celebrated Baby M), "gestational surrogates" will agree to carry and give birth to a baby to whom they bear no genetic relation whatsoever. It is now possible for a person to "have" a baby by procuring eggs and sperm from donors and hiring a "birth mother" to do the rest (this has been done). It is possible for a woman to use a birth mother for cosmetic reasons or convenience alone (this has also been done). It is possible for the sperm of dead men to be retrieved and used to impregnate their widows (likewise). It is possible for women long past the age of menopause to give birth (this, too, has already happened).

Egg Freezing

Another exceptional birth captured headlines in October 1997, when a woman whose ovaries were nonfunctional delivered two healthy boys courtesy of Reproductive Biology Associates in Atlanta. RBA had engineered the twins' conception using donor eggs frozen for more than two years. Because the sheer size and complexity of the human egg make it more susceptible than sperm to damage during freezing, protocols for the cryopreservation of eggs have been difficult to perfect. Until recently, in fact, most attempts at egg freezing have failed. The twins are the first of their kind to be born in the United States.

Though RBA's achievement was quickly overshadowed by the arrival of the Iowa septuplets, the egg-freezing feat has more significant ramifications. Once it becomes widely available, cryopreservation will offer a unique opportunity to women: the chance to store their young eggs for use at a later date. Defects in aging eggs are thought to be responsible for the de-

> *"Richard Seed, a physician turned fertility entrepreneur, [is] seeking funds to establish a laboratory for the cloning of adult human beings."*

clining fertility of older women; indeed, donor-egg technology has demonstrated that the rest of the female reproductive apparatus withstands the test of time. By assuring women a lifetime of viable gametes, egg freezing could let them beat the biological clock.

Of course, women would then be using assisted reproduction for their own convenience rather than for treatment of an existing medical condition. In this respect, egg freezing echoes a common theme in assisted reproduction. Current techniques were developed to help patients with specific medical problems— egg freezing, for example, will allow cancer patients whose eggs would be destroyed by radiation to set aside some gametes prior to therapy. Yet inevitably, the fruits of infertility research expand reproductive options for all men and women. And these choices are not always easy to live with, for individuals or for society.

Cloning Technology

A striking example comes from the laboratory of reproductive endocrinologist Jamie Grifo at New York University Medical Center. In another effort to beat the biological clock, Grifo is transferring the nuclei from older women's eggs into younger eggs from which the nuclei have been removed—that is, enucleated eggs. When these hybrid cells are artificially stimulated to divide, the transferred nuclei don't show the chromosomal abnormalities typical of vintage eggs. Grifo's work is still in the research stage, but he hopes eventually to fertilize such eggs and implant them in his patients.

"St. Barnabas Medical Center, a fertility clinic in Livingston, New Jersey, has begun offering young women $5,000 to donate eggs."

Grifo is not cloning humans, but his experiments draw on established mammalian cloning technology. Lamb 6LL3, better known as Dolly, was created by nuclear transfer from an adult cell to an enucleated egg. Grifo emphasizes that he's concerned only with transfers between egg cells for the purpose of treating infertility; he says he is strongly opposed to human cloning, and that in any case it will take years for researchers to figure out how to do it. "But the fact is, it's possible," he says. "I just can't think of any clinical indications for it."

If Grifo can't, someone else can. Richard Seed, a physicist turned infertility entrepreneur, made headlines in January 1998 when he announced that he was seeking funds to establish a laboratory for the cloning of adult human beings.

The National Bioethics Advisory Commission recommended a ban on human cloning back when Dolly first saw daylight. President Bill Clinton reiterated his call for a five-year moratorium on human cloning research. But the American Society for Reproductive Medicine, which issues ethical guidelines for the use of assisted-reproduction technologies, has taken the middle ground. "We do not support the cloning of an existing—or previously existing—individual," says Younger. "But that is not to say that cloning technology is bad." Cultures of cloned nerve cells, for example, could be used to treat spinal-cord injuries, he says. "We would not like to see research curtailed.". . .

An Unregulated Industry

Lack of regulation only exacerbates the problems surrounding assisted reproduction. "This field is screaming for regulation, oversight, and control," says Arthur Caplan, a noted bioethicist at the University of Pennsylvania. "What keeps us from doing so is the notion that individuals should have procreative freedom."

Rancor over abortion has also impeded the regulation of technologies for assisted reproduction. Since the 1970s, the United States has outlawed federal funding of research on human embryos or fetal tissue in response to concerns that such research would encourage trafficking in embryos and fetuses. The ban has not been applied to privately funded efforts, however; consequently, most research on assisted reproduction has been conducted beyond the reach of federal regulation and oversight.

Specialists in assisted reproduction, including Grifo, say this is just as well—that regulators wouldn't appreciate the technical and moral complexities of the work. But with the bulk of experimentation going on in private clinics, patients—and their children—can become guinea pigs. Even when couples are not directly involved in experimental procedures, they may be confronted with uncomfortable choices, such as financial incentives to donate their gametes or embryos.

"People often feel compelled by the circumstances—'What else could we do?'" says Barbara Katz Rothman, professor of sociology at Baruch College. "I'm not sure how we should make these decisions, but I'm pretty sure they shouldn't be made by the market."

And market forces affect more than just infertile couples. Although eggs are far more scarce and difficult to obtain than sperm, young women donors are typically given minimal compensation for their time and trouble. But in February 1998 the *New York Times* reported that St. Barnabas Medical Center, a fertility clinic in Livingston, New Jersey, has begun offering young women $5,000 to donate eggs—a price reported to be twice that of competitors. Unlike payment for organs, which is illegal, limited payment for eggs is legal. The professional guidelines of the American Society for Reproductive Medicine deem them "body products," not "body parts."

The Children of Assisted Reproduction

Many observers fear that it is not the participants in assisted reproduction but their children who may suffer most from the imprudent use of these new technologies. For example, with the rising popularity of assisted reproduction, more and more children are being exposed to the risks of premature birth: since 1971 the annual number of multiple births in the United States has more than quadrupled. Scientists and ethicists alike have spoken out against helping single, postmenopausal mothers conceive, arguing that it is morally reprehensible to create children who may well be orphaned. Some question the wisdom of arrangements—like surrogacy or gamete donation—that could diffuse the responsibility of parenthood. And some researchers are concerned with the safety of the procedures themselves for assisted reproduction. A recent—and controversial—Australian study of 420 children suggests that babies produced with the aid of intracytoplasmic sperm injection, in which a single sperm is injected into an incubating egg cell, are twice as likely to suffer major birth defects of the heart, genitals, and digestive tract.

"Many observers fear that it is not the participants in assisted reproduction but their children who may suffer most from the imprudent use of these new technologies."

"Everything we do in vitro to a mammalian embryo causes it stress," says

Robert Edwards, the specialist who presided over the first test-tube baby in 1978. "But there's immense responsibility in the scientific community" to evaluate and eliminate any adverse consequences of new procedures, he says.

Other commentators note that the rights of participants and progeny in assisted reproduction are still undefined. Laws vary widely from state to state on whether a child conceived by donor insemination has the right to know the identity of her biological father. "We never resolved the issues surrounding artificial insemination," says George Annas, a professor of law, medicine, and public health at Boston University. "We just act like we did. And then we import these issues into the new technology."

With the rapid advances in assisted-reproduction techniques, the ethical and legal issues can only become more complicated, and the task of resolving them will fall to future generations. But that may be fitting, if it's the children of assisted reproduction who pass judgment on the technology that helped create them.

Reproductive Technologies Are a Valid Medical Treatment

by Diane D. Aronson

About the author: *Diane D. Aronson is executive director of Resolve: The National Fertility Association, a nonprofit consumer advocacy group.*

What is the most important concern in your life.? For many people, the answer would be family. If you are a couple with a vision of building a family, the condition of infertility can interrupt this basic human desire. Infertility is a life-changing crisis that affects more than 10 percent of the reproductive-age population in the United States. Having children and raising a family, which comes easily to many couples, can be a heartbreaking challenge for those afflicted with infertility.

Infertility is a disease of the reproductive system which affects both men and women; it is not elective or selective. It strikes people in all walks of life, and it crosses racial, ethnic, religious and socioeconomic boundaries. Couples who experience infertility most often have to pay out of pocket for their diagnoses and treatments. Health-insurance coverage usually either is nonexistent or minimal.

Treatment Is Available

For many couples, only medical treatment can enable them to become pregnant and have children. While adoption is an option for many, the costs can reach $30,000, and there are not enough babies available in the United States to meet the need. Proven medical treatments are available, and insurance coverage should be provided as it is for other diseases. Insurance covers the maternal and neonatal costs for fertile couples who are able to have children. Individuals with infertility pay into the insurance plans that cover those costs, even though they often cannot access care to bear children. Couples who need medical assistance should not be denied the opportunity to become pregnant and have children.

In any given month, a normally fertile couple has a 22 percent chance of becoming pregnant. Nearly two-thirds of couples receiving infertility treatments have successful pregnancies. Most who successfully obtain medical assistance for infertility are able to do so through relatively low-cost ($500 to $2,000) and noninvasive treatments such as medication or intrauterine insemination.

Approximately 5 percent of couples who seek treatment undergo assisted reproductive technology, or ART, such as in vitro fertilization, which costs approximately $12,000 per attempt. When the woman has blocked fallopian tubes or the man has a low sperm count, ART treatment may be the only method by which a couple can become pregnant. Another treatment option is surgery, which usually costs more than ART but often is covered by insurance plans. Because of this coverage, couples may undergo multiple surgical procedures, even if ART would be the best and most cost-effective option. Such partial coverage encourages inefficiency and, at times, incorrect treatment choices. Insurance coverage of the range of treatments would allow for better management of care, as physicians and patients could then better determine the most effective treatment path.

Preventing Multiple Births

Infertility insurance coverage also would help to manage the rate of multiple births that result from some treatments. The multiple-birth rate among those who obtain infertility treatments is higher than among the general population. The neonatal costs following multiple births are high, as are the health risks to the mother and the babies. (The neonatal costs of the Chukwu octuplet births in Houston on Dec. 20, 1998, are estimated to be more than $2 million.)

When couples are struggling to have a child and do not have insurance coverage, they may be more willing to take risks in treatment that increase their chances of having a pregnancy but also could increase the chances of having a multiple birth. When paying out of pocket, knowing that they will not be able to afford more than a certain number of treatments affects their decisions and their willingness to take risks. Insurance coverage would remove that incentive. Further, insurance coverage would bring about additional oversight and management of care from the insurance company, which could in turn reduce the rate of multiple births. A 1998 study, led by physician David Frankfurter of Beth Israel Deaconess Medical Center in Boston, found that in states with mandated infertility-insurance coverage the average number of embryos transferred in an in vitro fertilization attempt was lower and the multiple-birth rate per attempt was lower than in states without mandates. The study's authors concluded that this lower rate of multiple births may be a result of less pressure from patients to maximize the chance of pregnancy and increased pressure from insurers to minimize the likelihood of multiple births.

"Infertility is a disease of the reproductive system."

Infertility Is a Disability Like Any Other

Couples who experience infertility ride an emotional roller coaster—from diagnosis through treatment—a very difficult experience. The physical and emotional struggles are further exacerbated when couples face financial hurdles because of a lack of insurance coverage. Alice D. Domar of the Mind/Body Institute at Beth Israel Deaconess Medical Center led a study of women with chronic diseases which found that the psychological effect of experiencing infertility was similar to that of cancer and heart disease. Compounding the emotional distress is the stigma of infertility and the difficulty that many couples have in telling their family and friends.

What is fair when it comes to insurance coverage? The Supreme Court strengthened the arguments in favor of infertility-insurance coverage when it issued a ruling in June 1998 that demonstrated the importance of reproduction and the ability to have children. In *Bragdon vs. Abbott* the high court ruled that reproduction is a major life activity under the Americans with Disabilities Act, or ADA. According to the ADA, an individual is disabled if he or she has a mental or physical impairment that substantially limits one or more major life activities. Therefore, those who are impaired in their ability to reproduce may qualify for protection from discrimination based on that disability. This ruling allows those experiencing infertility to make claims of discrimination when employers specifically exclude infertility treatment from insurance plans. A number of lawsuits have arisen in the wake of that decision.

> *"Couples who need medical assistance should not be denied the opportunity to become pregnant and have children."*

While Bragdon was not a case involving infertility (the plaintiff was an HIV-positive woman who was denied dental care), lower courts have ruled in cases specific to infertility that it qualifies as a disability under the ADA. In *Bielicki vs. The City of Chicago*, police officers Anita and Vince Bielicki sued the city of Chicago for excluding infertility treatment from their health plans. After the U.S. District Court for the Northern District of Illinois ruled that reproduction is a major life activity and that the Bielickis' lawsuit could go forward, the city decided to settle. Most infertility-treatment costs incurred by employees in the previous 10 years were reimbursed, and city health-insurance plans now include infertility coverage. The precedents set by this case and the Supreme Court ruling, and the prospect of further lawsuits, have brought infertility-insurance coverage to the attention of a growing number of employers and legislators.

The Costs Are Low

William M. Mercer, a benefits consulting firm, published a report in 1997 which disclosed that approximately 25 percent of employers provide some infertility insurance coverage. Another consulting firm, the Segal Co., issued an

August 1998 report which found that only 7 percent of employer plans cover infertility treatment, and about 14 percent of plans cover the costs of infertility diagnosis. Most of those plans that cover treatment do not cover all infertility services.

The costs of including infertility coverage in an insurance plan are low. Studies cited by the Mercer report found that the cost of in vitro fertilization coverage is approximately $2.50 per member per year. Another study, by Martha Griffin and William F. Panak, published in the July 1998 issue of *Fertility and Sterility*, found that the cost of comprehensive infertility coverage is $1.71 per family plan per month. Isn't it worth the cost of a monthly cup of coffee to ensure that couples who are struggling to build much-wanted families are afforded the option?

> *"Helping couples who are struggling to build much-wanted families is the right thing to do."*

State Infertility Insurance Laws

Several state legislatures have responded to the needs of their constituents and recognized the importance of supporting couples who are striving to build their families. Thirteen states enacted infertility insurance laws after they determined that such financial assistance is in the best interest of their residents. The mandates are quite different in scope and substance. Ten states have a mandate to provide some level of infertility insurance. Three states have a mandate to offer under which insurance companies must have infertility insurance available for purchase, but employers do not have to choose to provide that coverage to their employees.

A number of state legislatures considered infertility-insurance laws in the 1997–98 legislative session, and new legislation is being drafted for introduction in 1999. Mandates may be introduced in Florida, Indiana, Michigan, Nevada, New Hampshire, New Jersey, New York, Pennsylvania, Tennessee and Texas. Infertility patients, providers and others who understand the need for insurance coverage are working to gather support for mandates, and a number of legislators have committed to assist.

The Need for a Federal Infertility Insurance Mandate

The existing infertility-insurance mandates have allowed many couples to obtain needed medical treatments and to build their families. However, even in states with mandates, many employees still do not have insurance coverage because of the Employee Retirement Income Security Act, or ERISA. Employers who self-insure are exempt from any state health-insurance mandates, including infertility mandates. In some states, more than 50 percent of employees work for exempted employers. Self-insured employers sometimes do choose to follow the state's policy lead and provide infertility coverage to their employees.

A federal infertility insurance mandate, a long-term goal of the infertility community, would cover all employers and make coverage consistent across states.

Legislators and employers are beginning to recognize that helping couples who are struggling to build much-wanted families is the right thing to do. In a country that places great value in family, it is salutary that insurance coverage for couples with infertility is just around the corner.

Reproductive Technologies Can Be Consistent with Christian Beliefs

by Elvonne Whitney

About the author: *Elvonne Whitney is a physician specializing in obstetrics, gynecology, and assisted reproductive techniques. She is a member of the American Society for Reproductive Medicine and is on the faculty at Loma Linda University School of Medicine in Loma Linda, California.*

The struggle many infertile Christian couples face in their quest for a child is one that God is certainly sensitive to. Many Biblical examples, including that of Hannah, attest to His caring, concern, and at times, intervention for those who desire an offspring. Many more couples than previously now have the opportunity to have their desired child using assisted reproduction technologies. However, these technologies raise important ethical and moral questions, and Christian couples and the health care providers assisting them do well to seek God's will in these areas. The church can also seek to assist such individuals in their understanding of God's will.

While most of this discussion will apply to any infertile couple, some of the issues discussed apply most specifically to those considering in vitro fertilization, egg or sperm donation, or the use of a surrogate mother.

Christians Value Individual Freedom of Choice

First of all, let us remember how important individual freedom of choice is to God. I have seen many couples who struggle with much pain because of other family members' or church members' behavior and comments regarding their decision to use various assisted reproductive technologies. Some choose not to share their struggle or decisions with others because of such hurtful behavior, and as a result often feel very isolated. Some struggle with guilt, feeling that their difficulty conceiving a child is a result of past sins, and God is punishing them. Our

Reprinted from Elvonne Whitney, "Assisted Reproduction: A Christian Clinician's View," at www.surrogacy.com/medres/article/christv.html, October 1996, by permission of the American Surrogacy Center.

God is a forgiving God, and whatever past acts may have been done, He views His children with compassion and forgiveness. The church should be a place where all such couples can receive support and compassion in their struggle.

The decision to use or not use such technologies is a deeply personal one, to be settled between a couple and God. The church family should value and protect each couple's individual privacy and decision in these matters, while offering comfort, understanding, and careful support in their seeking of God's will for those who choose to share their struggle.

For issues where no clear Biblical instructions exist, we must support individuals in their personal interpretation and application of the principles involved. We must tread very carefully in this area. God can speak to individuals just as easily, and perhaps more so, than He can speak to organizations in areas of such personal concern. This is not to negate the role of the community of faith in assisting couples in their struggle with these questions, or to limit the importance of the principles involved. But perhaps we do best to outline the issues and principles, and support individuals in their own application of them. Any creation of a "rule book" would go against the way God deals with His people in these personal areas.

The Importance of Family

Now let us consider some specific points. There certainly is clear scriptural support for a child having the benefits of a stable family. This is helpful in making a decision to limit the application of assisted reproductive technologies to married couples. A number of European countries have outlawed assisted reproduction for unmarried individuals on purely secular grounds.

However, there is a vast difference between using these technologies on unmarried individuals, and in applying such technologies to couples where one or both partners is unable to either produce eggs or sperm, or carry a pregnancy. Let us consider that heritage is composed of multiple factors. Genetic heritage is important, but not necessarily the most important. Social and spiritual heritage are vital as well. This is illustrated in several scriptural examples. Among these is the Old Testament Levirate rule, whereby if a man died with no heirs, his brother was to, in today's terms, inseminate his wife "so his name may not be blotted out of Israel." In essence, this was God's direction for the use of sperm donation to carry on the family line if an individual had no children.

> *"The decision to use or not use [reproductive] technologies is a deeply personal one, to be settled between a couple and God."*

Another example: both Rachel and Leah had sons for Jacob using their maids Bilhah and Zilpah. This has many similarities to today's surrogate mothers. Also, Abraham used Hagar to produce an offspring because of Sarah's infertility. Though this caused problems later because of rivalry, etc., between the two women, God did not forbid it. While the specifics in these examples may be said to relate to the Hebrew culture, and other principles are illustrated here also, it does indicate God's appreciation for man's need to pass his social and spiritual heritage on to his offspring even if he cannot pass on his genetic heritage. God has created within human beings a desire to procreate and fulfill His original mandate to "Be fruitful and multiply." There may be instances where social and spiritual heritage are more important than genetic heritage.

Respect for Human Life

There is no doubt that the use of assisted reproductive technologies raises difficult ethical questions. However, shouldn't Christians be in a better position than others to speak to these questions in the light of scripture and the Holy Spirit's guidance? We would do well to expend effort in understanding the issues the use of donor sperm or oocytes and surrogacy raise, and in developing effective ways to assist couples in dealing with these issues if they so choose, rather then summarily recommending avoiding them.

Human life must be treated with respect at all stages of development. This is Biblical. Any Christian couple should carefully consider ahead of time the moral issues regarding such things as the number of ova to be fertilized with in vitro fertilization, and the disposition of remaining pre-embryos. Simply discarding "unused" embryos does not follow Biblical principles

> *"As with any technology or power, we must use our growing understanding of human reproduction responsibly and under His guidance."*

regarding the sacredness of human life. The availability of cryo-preservation, or freezing, of such embryos is one alternative available. This can allow the couple to have further attempts at conception if the initial attempt fails. It may also allow the possibility of having more than one child, or the opportunity to donate such pre-embryos to another infertile couple who may be unable to have a child any other way. It is hoped that soon technology will allow us to freeze unfertilized oocytes, and this will make some of these decisions easier, in that only very few oocytes need be inseminated at one time and any remaining oocytes frozen for possible later use.

Another issue is that of multiple pregnancy. Current technologies significantly increase the chance for twins, triplets, and other multiple births. Because of the very high risk of severe prematurity and non-survival of babies from pregnancies with four or more fetuses, selective termination of one or more fetuses is available. This obviously raises important moral issues. Is it right to intentionally terminate one or more fetuses so that the remaining ones will have a significantly better chance for survival? Is it right to allow the pregnancy to continue with several fetuses, with the likelihood that no babies may survive?

Many see the Biblical imperative against voluntarily taking human life as an answer to this issue. Any decision is sure to be agonizing. Therefore, when using such technologies it is imperative to use every medical effort to minimize the possibility of multiple pregnancy so that such a decision will rarely need to be made. Thankfully, we can now control that risk to a large degree.

There are some other issues that any couple considering sperm or egg donation, or surrogacy, should prayerfully consider. These include the feelings of the wife and husband about a third party being involved in the conception of their child. There is also the question of whether and when to tell the child the details of his or her conception, and whether to tell family and friends. The couple will want to be sure all legal and medical questions are fully addressed. Also, many of these technologies are very expensive, and couples will want to be sure that they are using their financial resources wisely and in a way that God would approve.

Every Conception Is a Miracle

There are many things that medical technology can do with our current understanding of God's laws. There are also many things that we cannot do. A major example of this is that once embryos, eggs, or sperm are replaced in the uterus, we have no more control over their further development. Whether or not pregnancy occurs, and how many embryos continue to develop, is out of our hands. God is still in control, and every conception is a miracle. In a sense it is as though God has said, "This far you may come, and no farther."

Let me point to one more Biblical example of God's view of infertility. Throughout his walk with God, Abraham was repeatedly promised a son. This son would begin a line of descendants that would outnumber the stars of the heavens and eventually lead to Jesus Himself. God fulfilled His promise to Abraham in a miraculous way. While God may not choose to intervene miraculously in the lives of every infertile couple, He can certainly bless the efforts of Christian couples to have children using the technologies that our growing understanding of His wondrous ways allows. At times God has chosen to heal numerous physical diseases miraculously. However, He can also greatly bless the efforts of health care providers in applying our constantly growing knowledge to help heal disease and relieve suffering.

Should there be any fundamental difference between our view of other medical treatment and of Christians' search to fulfill one of their most basic God-given desires, that of having offspring? God is ultimately the Great Physician. I never cease to be amazed at His wondrous works each time conception occurs with or without assistance. As with any technology or power, we must use our growing understanding of human reproduction responsibly and under His guidance. And in doing so we can be partners with God in the joy of the recurring miracle of new life.

Multiple Births Are an Acceptable Consequence of Assisted Reproduction

by Marianne Moody Jennings

About the author: *Marianne Moody Jennings is a professor of legal and ethical studies at Arizona State University.*

With Guinness multiple births like the Iowa McCaughey septuplets or the Chukwu octuplets of Houston, gratitude emerges: "Better thee than we." Just the Huggies bills and colic necessitate a declaration of cruel and unusual punishment.

The Hypocrisy of Condemning Multiple Births

Also with these multiple births come medical ethicists and zero-population growthers (who since 1970 have been predicting Old Testament locust plagues if childbearing continued) with a rousing chorus of grinching. Their bemoaning of fecundity includes "irresponsible," "techno births" and "bizarre spectacle." Mention the word "miracle" around this crowd and you'll find yourself hot-glued with Binkys and driven from town on a Mattel Big Wheel.

Grinching is one of my favorite activities, but there is nothing so annoying as an inconsistent grinch. Questioning the abortion of a "fetus" is impermissible, for such is a woman's private choice. The converse, however, is inapplicable: The decision to continue life is neither private nor a choice. Mention that same-sex marriage could be a problem or that adultery reflects character and you will be condemned for the New Age capital offense of judgment. Condemning successful reproduction, however, has become avant-garde. Grinches bandy about multiple births as if discussing bougainvillea containment. Their feigned histrionics are based on tailored information with imported credibility and sincerity from medical ethics that capitalizes on the public's lack of information about infertility.

In the world of infertility, even with the most extreme procedures, the chances of multiple births are slim. I took the same drugs and underwent the

Reprinted from Marianne Moody Jennings, "Multiple-Birth Grinches Abort Facts, Bear Hypocrisy," *Arizona Republic*, January 10, 1999, www.azcentral.com, by permission of the author.

same procedures as Bobbi McCaughey and Nkem Chukwu but had single births each time, like 80 percent of my fellow infertilites (only 1 percent of mothers have more than triplets). Grinch myths aside, multiple births remain rare, and technology has triplet and quadruplet births conquered.

Contrary to the preposterous grinch assertions that these couples are naive, infertility specialists practice full disclosure and painful candor.

> *"Condemning successful reproduction . . . has become avant-garde."*

My husband and I knew risks, follicle counts and costs of everything from preemie care to diapers. Most relevantly, for purposes of dispelling grinch legends, we had these discussions and disclosures before we undertook any procedures, not when we were faced with seven follicles.

It is inconceivable, as it were, for grinches to fathom that a couple knowingly would undertake such risk. Infertile couples have a sincere but elusive and humiliating desire to have children. You can't do something teenagers accomplish with just one encounter in the back seat of a Geo: conception. Charles and Diana hated each other and did it, bank robbers have done it, even Geraldo. The adoption route finds you fingerprinted, investigated and questioned. Face a county social worker who shares your living room for three hours with questions such as the sine qua non of parent suitability—"What do you love best about Marianne?"—and septuplets look good. I challenge any married couple in America to answer that question without rehearsal and not produce Middle East–level tension.

The Financial Costs of Multiple Births Are Exaggerated

These couples are sentenced to a world not for the fainthearted. Grinches' fear of a stampede to infertility clinics is ill-founded, for most couples stop at Clomid tablets, lacking the fortitude for daily injections, frustration and no guarantees of success or its numbers. Infertility treatment is expensive, and insurers are not picking up the tab, as the grinches allege. Ninety percent of all employer-based health-insurance plans exclude coverage, and private insurance for such elective procedures is prohibitive.

We approached each injection and step with trepidation, but with a willingness to accept whatever fate brought us, because we hated the social workers and for one other reason articulated by Mrs. Chukwu: You take what God grants. Faith is a common denominator in infertility and multiple births. Regardless of success or failure, you come away with a profound appreciation for the miracle of life.

Much is made of what it costs to save these babies. In the past month, lawyers claimed fees of $30 billion in the tobacco settlement. Dow Corning will pay nearly $3 billion to women who thought breast enhancement would be fun and then cashed in on their silicone vanity with baseless claims. Springing for a couple of million ($2 million for the Chukwu babies) on infant life sounds positively intellectual in comparison. Indeed, villagers in Iowa and Houston have found joy in service and giving to these families. These multiple-birth children, though not on welfare rolls, are depicted as a societal burden, while millions of babies born singly to single mothers spend a lifetime as economic wards.

Miracle Births Are Not a Cause for Outrage

One medical ethicist asked, "Who benefits from eight babies? Nobody views eight as a success." I do. The Chukwus do. The year-old thriving McCaughey septuplets do. Non-judgmental society picks multiple births as the time for outrage. Raining on the parade of the infertile seems oddly incongruent in a world in which privacy and choice reign supreme. But it is consistent for a world in which cries for reform abound when faith and miracles rear their defiant heads.

Philosopher Josiah Royce described the role of faith in life and science: "It is difficult to wrestle with angels, but there are some blessings that cannot be won any other way." Seven or eight babies in one fell swoop is not an easy task, medically or physically, but these little angels offer a glimpse of theism in a detached world.

Cloning Can Be an Acceptable Means of Reproduction

by James Q. Wilson

About the author: *James Q. Wilson is Collins professor of management and public policy at the University of California Los Angeles and the author of several books, including* The Moral Sense *and* On Character: Essays.

Let us suppose that it becomes possible to clone human beings. The creation of Dolly the cloned sheep makes this more likely than anyone once suspected. How should we react to this event?

Like most people, I instinctively recoil from the idea. There is, I think, a natural sentiment that is offended by the mental picture of identical babies being produced in some biological factory. When we hear a beautiful model say that she would like to have a clone of herself, we are puzzled. When we recall *The Boys from Brazil,* a story of identical offspring of Adolf Hitler being raised in order to further his horrible work, we are outraged.

But before deciding what we think about cloning, we ought to pause and identify more precisely what it is about the process that is so distressing. My preliminary view is that the central problem is not creating an identical twin but creating it without parents.

Science Cannot Be Stopped

Happily, we need not react immediately to human cloning. The task of moving from one sheep to many sheep, and from sheep to other animals, and from animals to humans, will be long and difficult. Dolly was the only lamb to emerge out of 277 attempts, and we still do not know how long she will live or what diseases, if any, she might contract.

And the risks attendant on a hasty reaction are great. A premature ban on any scientific effort moving in the direction of cloning could well impede useful research on the genetic basis of diseases or on opportunities for improving agriculture. Already a great deal of work is underway on modifying the genetic structure of laboratory animals in order to study illnesses and to generate human proteins and antibodies. Aware of the value of genetic research, several members of Congress have expressed reservations about quick legislative action. Nevertheless, bills to ban cloning research have been introduced.

But even if such bills pass, the argument will be far from over. Congress may regulate or even block cloning research in the United States, but other countries are free to pursue their own strategies. If cloning is illegal in America but legal in Japan or China, Americans will go to those countries as cloning techniques are perfected. Science cannot be stopped. We should have learned this from the way we regulate drug treatments. We can ban a risky but useful drug, but the only effect is to limit its use to those who are willing and able to pay the airfare to Hong Kong.

Objections to Cloning

There are both philosophical and utilitarian objections to cloning. Two philosophical objections exist. The first is that cloning violates God's will by creating an infant in a way that does not depend on human sexual congress or make possible the divine inculcation of a soul. That is true, but so does in vitro fertilization. An egg and a sperm are united outside the human body in a glass container. The fertilized egg is then put into the body of either the woman who produced it or another woman hired to bear the infant. When first proposed, in vitro fertilization was ethically suspect. Today, it is generally accepted, and for good reason. Science supplies what one or both human bodies lack, namely, a reasonable chance to produce an infant. Surely God can endow that infant with a soul. Cloning, of course, removes one of the conjugal partners, but it is hard to imagine that God's desire to bestow a unique soul can be blocked by the fact that the infant does not result from an egg and sperm's joining but instead arises from an embryonic egg's reproducing itself.

The other philosophical objection is that cloning is contrary to nature. This is often asserted by critics of cloning who do not believe in an active God. I sympathize with this reaction, but few critics have yet made clear to me what compelling aspect of nature cloning violates. To the extent this objection has meaning, I think it

> *"The central problem [with human cloning] is not creating an identical twin but creating it without parents."*

must arise from the danger that the cloned child will be put to various harmful uses. If so, it cannot easily be distinguished from the more practical problems.

One set of those problems requires us to imagine scientists' cloning children in order to harvest organs and body parts or producing for later use many Adolf Hitlers or Saddam Husseins. I have no doubt that there will arise mad scientists willing to do these things. After all, they have already created poison gas and conducted grisly experiments on prisoners of war and concentration-camp inmates.

Ensuring That Cloned Children Have Parents Will Prevent Abuse

But under what circumstances will such abuses occur? Largely, I think, when the cloned child has no parents. Parents, whether they acquire a child by normal birth, artificial insemination, or adoption, will, in the overwhelming majority of cases, become deeply attached to the infant and care for it without regard to its origin. The parental tie is not infallible—infanticide occurs, and some neonates are abandoned in trash bins—but it is powerful and largely independent of the origin of the child. If cloning is to occur, the central problem is to ensure that it be done only for two-parent families who want a child for their own benefit. We should remember that a clone must be borne by a female; it cannot be given birth in a laboratory. A human mother will carry a human clone; she and her husband will determine its fate. Hardly any parents, I think, would allow their child to be used as an organ bank for defective adults or as the next-generation proxy for a malevolent dictator. If the cloned child is born in the same way as a child resulting from marital congress, can it matter to the parents how it was conceived? And if it does not matter to the parents, should it matter to us?

We already have a kind of clone: identical twins. They are genetically identical humans. I have not heard of any twin's being used against its will as an unwitting organ bank for its brother or sister. Some may surrender

> *"If cloning is to occur, the central problem is to ensure that it be done only for two-parent families who want a child for their own benefit."*

a kidney or bone marrow to their sibling; many may give blood; but none, I think, has been "harvested." The idea that a cloned infant, born to its mother, would be treated differently is, I think, quite far-fetched.

At some time in the future, science may discover a way to produce a clone entirely in the laboratory. That we should ban. Without human birth, the parents' attitude toward the infant will be deeply compromised. Getting a clone from a laboratory would be like getting a puppy from a pet store: Both creatures might be charming, but neither would belong in any meaningful emotional sense to the owner. And unclaimed clones would be disposed of the same way as unclaimed puppies—killed.

There may be parents who, out of fear or ideology, can be persuaded to accept a clone of a Hussein in hopes that they can help produce an unending chain of vicious leaders. This is less far-fetched. We already know from the study of identical twins reared in different families that they are remarkably similar. A cloned Hussein would have an IQ close to that of his father and a personality that (insofar as we can measure these things) would have roughly a 50 percent chance of being like his. Each clone would be like an identical twin:

nearly the same in appearance, very similar in intelligence and manner, and alike (but not a duplicate) in personality. We know that the environment will have some effect on each twin's personality, but it is easy to overestimate this. I am struck by how many scientists interested in cloning have reflexively adopted the view that the environment will have a powerful effect on a cloned child. (Cloning seems to have given a large boost to environmentalists.) But that reaction is exaggerated.

> *"Cloning guarantees that the child's genetic makeup will be identical to that of whichever parent is cloned."*

From the work of Dr. Thomas Bouchard at the University of Minnesota, we know that giving identical twins different environments produces only slightly greater differences in character.

Our best hope for guarding against the duplication of a Saddam Hussein is a practical one. Any cloned offspring would reach maturity 40 or so years after his father was born, and by then so much would have changed—Hussein, Sr. would probably not even be in power, and his country's political system might have been profoundly altered—that it is unlikely Hussein, Jr. could do what his father did.

Cloning as a Solution for Infertile Couples

We do not know how many parents will request cloning, but some will. Suppose the father cannot provide sperm or the mother is unable to produce a fertilizable egg. Such a family now has only two choices—remain childless or adopt. Cloning would create a third choice: duplicate the father or the mother. Some parents who do not want to remain childless will find this more attractive than adoption, which introduces a wholly new and largely unknown genetic factor into their family tree. Cloning guarantees that the child's genetic makeup will be identical to that of whichever parent is cloned.

There is, of course, a risk that cloning may increase the number of surrogate mothers, with all of the heartbreak and legal complexities that this entails, but I suspect that surrogates would be no more common for clones than they are for babies conceived in vitro.

More troubling is the possibility that a lesbian couple will use cloning to produce a child. Do we wish to make it easy for a homosexual pair to have children? Governments have different policies on this; let me set aside discussion of this matter for another occasion.

Evolutionary Aspects of Cloning

There is one important practical objection to the widespread use of cloning. As every evolutionary scientist knows, the survival of a species depends on two forces—environmental change that rewards some creatures and penalizes others, and sufficient diversity among the species that no matter what the environment, some members of the species will benefit.

Cloning creates the opportunity for people to maximize a valued trait. Suppose we wish to have children with a high IQ, an athletic physique, easily tanned skin, or freedom from a particular genetic disease. By cloning persons who have the desired trait, we can guarantee that the trait will appear in the infant.

This may make good sense to parents, but it is bad news for the species. We have no way of knowing what environmental challenges will confront us in the future. Traits that today are desirable may become irrelevant or harmful in the future; traits that now are unappealing may become essential for human survival in the centuries ahead.

This problem is one for which there is no obvious individual solution. People maximizing the welfare of their infant can inhibit the welfare of the species. One way to constrain a couple's efforts to secure the "perfect" child would be to restrict their choice of genes to either the father or the mother. They could secure a specific genetic product, but they could not obtain what they might think is the ideal product.

The Allure of Uncertainty

But the real constraint on the misuse of cloning comes from a simple human tendency. Many parents do not want a child with particular traits. Conception is a lottery. It produces an offspring that gets roughly half of its genes from its father and half from its mother, but the mixture occurs in unpredictable and fascinating combinations. All parents spend countless delightful hours wondering whether the child has its mother's eyes or its father's smile or its grandfather's nose or its grandmother's personality. And they watch in wonder as the infant becomes an adult with its own unique personality and mannerisms.

I think that most people prefer the lottery to certainty. (I know they prefer sex to cloning.) Lured by the lottery, they help meet the species' need for biological diversity. Moreover, if parents are tempted by certainty but limited to cells taken from either the father or the mother, they will have to ask themselves hard questions.

Do I want another man like the father, who is smart and earns a lot—but whose hair is receding, who has diabetes, and who is so obsessed with work that he is not much fun on weekends? Or do I want another woman like the mother, who is bright and sweet—but who has bad teeth, a family risk of breast cancer, and sleeps too late in the morning?

Not many of us know perfect people, least of all our own parents. If we want to clone a person, most of us will think twice about cloning somebody we already know well. And if we can clone only from among our own family, our desire to do it at all will be much weakened. Perhaps parents' love of entering the reproductive lottery is itself a revelation of evolution at work, one designed to help maintain biological diversity.

In one special case we may want to clone a creature well known to us. My friend Heather Higgins has said that cloning our pets—or at least some pets—may make sense. I would love to have another Labrador retriever just like Winston and another pair of cats exactly like Sarah and Clementine.

Weighing Risks and Benefits

The central question facing those who approach cloning with an open mind is whether the gains from human cloning—a remedy for infertility and substitute for adoption—are worth the risks of farming organs, propagating dictators, and impeding evolution. I think that, provided certain conditions are met, the gains will turn out to exceed the risks.

The conditions are those to which I have already referred. Cloning should be permitted only on behalf of two married partners, and the mother should—absent some special medical condition that doctors must certify—carry the fertile tissue to birth. Then the offspring would belong to the parents. This parental constraint would prevent organ farming and the indiscriminate or political misuse of cloning technology.

The major threat cloning produces is a further weakening of the two-parent family. Cloning humans, if it can occur at all, cannot be prevented, but cloning unmarried persons will expand the greatest cultural problem our country now faces. A cloned child, so far as we now know, cannot be produced in a laboratory. A mother must give it birth. Dolly had a mother, and if humans are produced the same way, they will have mothers, also. But not, I hope, unmarried mothers. Indeed, given the likely expense and difficulty of cloning, and the absence from it of any sexual pleasure, we are unlikely to see many unmarried teenage girls choosing that method. If unmarried cloning occurs, it is likely to be among affluent persons who think they are entitled to act without the restraints and burdens of family life. They are wrong.

Of course an unmarried or unscrupulous person eager for a cloned offspring may travel from the United States to a place where there are no restrictions of the sort I suggest. There is no way to prevent this. We can try to curtail it by telling anyone

> *"If unmarried cloning occurs, it is likely to be among affluent persons who think they are entitled to act without the restraints and burdens of family life. They are wrong."*

who returns to this country with a child born abroad to an American citizen that one of two conditions must be met before the child will be regarded as an American citizen. The parent bringing it back must show by competent medical evidence either that the child is the product of a normal (non-cloned) birth or adoption or that the child, though the product of cloning, belongs to a married couple who will be responsible for it. Failing this, the child could not become an American citizen. But of course some people would evade any restrictions.

There is, in short, no way that American law can produce a fail-safe restraint on undesirable cloning.

Religious Objections Remain

My view—that cloning presents no special ethical risks if society does all in its power to establish that the child is born to a married woman and is the joint responsibility of the married couple—will not satisfy those whose objections to cloning are chiefly religious. If man is made in the image of God, can man make himself (by cloning) and still be in God's image? I would suggest that producing a fertilized egg by sexual contact does not uniquely determine that image and therefore that non-sexual, in vitro fertilization is acceptable. And if this is so, then non-sexually transplanting cell nuclei into enucleated eggs might also be acceptable.

This is not a view that will commend itself to many devout Christians or Jews. I would ask of them only that they explain what it is about sexual fertilization that so affects God's judgment about the child that results.

Reproductive Technologies Are Morally Problematic

by Jacqueline Laing

About the author: *Jacqueline Laing is a lawyer, lecturer, and free-lance jour-nalist in London, England. She completed her doctorate in moral and legal philosophy at Brasenose College, University of Oxford.*

It is over 20 years since the birth of Louise Brown, the first test-tube baby. Photographs of chubby toddlers transforming into attractive women persuade us to accept the totality of the new reproductive technologies. Indeed the con-sulting room walls of renowned experts in the field, such as the much-televised Professors Robert Winston and Ian Craft, bristle with photographs of their young creations and grateful commissioning parents. And it is hard not to wel-come a vision of this sort. But the reality behind these undeniably appealing images must give us pause.

An Industry That Manufactures Babies

In 20 years, a new multi-million pound industry has sprung up, offering in many cases not merely to cure infertility but to circumvent the problem by man-ufacturing a baby to satisfy the desires of commissioning parties.

GIFT (gamete intra-fallopian transfer) places sperm and ova into the fallopian tube in an attempt to fertilise them there. IVF mixes eggs collected from the woman's body with sperm in a petri dish to fertilise them and place them in the uterus.

Both techniques mimic and replace old-fashioned sex through the introduc-tion of a middle man. His place is to create human life; sometimes to freeze it, sometimes to experiment on it, and in many cases to destroy it. Gametes (i.e. sperm and ova), as well as human embryos, are routinely frozen and kept in banks where they are able to survive for decades.

In 1932 Aldous Huxley [author of *Brave New World*] described the fictitious "Central London Hatchery and Conditioning Centre", 600 years in the future. He wrote of "bulging flanks row upon row and tier above tier of bottles", of

Reprinted from Jacqueline Laing, "What's Love Got to Do with It?" *The Independent*, July 21, 1998, by permission of the author.

numbered test tubes of male gametes kept at 35 degrees and the female kept at 37, and of the fertilising process which inspected gametes for abnormalities and transferred them to a porous receptacle for fertilisation with sperm and sent back to incubators.

The powerful image was of a production process, of the manufacture of quality-controlled children for a brave new world. And it is this production process that is the real trou-

> *"Reproductive technologies are, of their very nature, morally problematic."*

ble with this new burgeoning industry in 1998. In essence, we have the mass storage that Huxley described, and children produced through IVF are often screened for abnormalities.

Treating Children as Commodities

Assisted reproduction is a hornet's nest. What is fundamentally at issue is the child and women's fertility. By interfering in the reproductive act, the technologists behave as though very young humans are just commodities, to be created, maintained and destroyed (if "unfit for their purpose") to satisfy the desires of desperate couples.

Children are being treated as if they were mere commodities to which commissioning parties have a right, whether by private funding or by virtue of the National Health Service. Like commodities they are subject to quality-control tests. But should we think of young human beings as if they were manufactured entities and women's fertility as a form of product manufacture?

Parental obligation and natural parental fondness are necessarily involved in the generation of human beings in a way that is not necessary in product manufacture. Again, commodities may be regarded as expendable if they are not fit for their purpose in a way that human beings ought not. Additionally, children have a sense of identity and often need to know from where they came; whereas merchandise makes no such demand.

Questionable Practices

Anonymous gamete donation is only one aspect of the new reproductive technologies that fails to accord the respect that is due to the child. Well-intentioned though gamete donors may be, they are essentially abandoning responsibility, both emotional and financial, for their children.

Furthermore, given the commercial and scientific interests at stake, it is quite possible for the modern clinician to prey on the unjustified fears of some women that their lives are meaningless or unfulfilled unless they have children. The truth, without labouring the point, is that one can lead a good and fulfilling life without children.

Examples of the manufacturing madness of the new bio-technocrats are legion. One British bio-technology expert and pioneer has inseminated human eggs into rabbits and monkeys in an effort to fertilise them there. He and others have called for further experimentation with human embryos in pigs, sheep and rabbits. Rats' ova have been crossed with human sperm. Hamster tests, (examinations which test the motility or vigour of men's sperm by attempting fertilisation in hamster's ovum), are often used in IVF programmes.

It is now possible to freeze gametes and embryos and, consequently, to create human beings whose parents are long dead. A child can be created using the sperm of a corpse and the egg of a dead foetus. And cloning introduces the possibility of asexual reproduction.

News of the use of corpses in IVF in the United States suggests that there are no limits to which the clinician will go to satisfy the desires of those they deem meritorious. Dr Cappy Rothman, the urologist who undertook this and other sperm extractions believes that his work "gives people hope and lessens the pain of suddenly losing a loved one".

People can now regard death as no barrier to the production of children and grandchildren they never had. There is no question that sperm and ova frozen today can, in principle, be used to generate children 50 years hence.

Reproductive Technologies Are Open to Abuse

Fertility clinic malpractice exists too. Couples and women at a fertility clinic in California who agreed to freeze their embryos returned to discover that their embryos or eggs had been given to other infertile couples who had gone on to bear their genetic offspring.

Examples of test-tube mix-ups abound. One white couple, after having undergone fertility treatment, thought they were going to have their own genetic child, only to discover that the mother had given birth to a bouncing black baby girl. Unhappy with their "product", the white couple then decided to sue.

Ian Craft may assert that it is "not [their] place to moralise", but the view that it is a doctor's place simply to consider, and attempt to satisfy, the desires of his patients shrouds the fact that reproductive technologies are, of their very nature, morally problematic.

> "*Anonymous gamete donation is only one aspect of the new reproductive technologies that fails to accord the respect that is due to the child.*"

Just because a patient wants something does not necessarily imply that he or she should have it. A man who wants to father hosts of children with different women, who themselves agree to artificial insemination using anonymous donor sperm, should not necessarily have his desire accommodated. There are moral limits to what can be legitimately undertaken and patient desires are not always paramount.

Indeed the above example is not as far-fetched as it may seem. There is a fertility expert in Virginia who has been tried for providing his own sperm to at least 15 couples. Many more couples chose, for obvious reasons, not to give evidence against him.

This is, of course, a case of fertility malpractice. But what the example is designed to challenge is the extent to which a medical practitioner can be said to be a mere technician simply giving effect to the desires of his patients.

The Moral Questions Surrounding
Assisted Reproduction Must Be Addressed

In the 20 years since Louise Brown was born, IVF and related technologies have become commonplace. Behind the facade of picturesque toddlers there are underlying moral conundrums which are still not being addressed.

In such a rapidly developing field, the morality of the new reproductive technologies should be considered before they become reality. If we fail to do this, we will then risk becoming a society that is insensitive to the duties that it unquestionably owes to its innocent members, and instead prefers to develop and cater to the manufacturing zeal of the new bio-technocrats.

Some Reproductive Technologies Violate Christian Beliefs

by Daniel McConchie

About the author: *Daniel McConchie is operations coordinator and director of development for the Center for Bioethics and Human Dignity, an educational organization that works to bring a Christian perspective to contemporary issues in bioethics.*

The inability to have a child is a true burden. Would-be parents often ask both God and themselves why their innate desire to have children continues to be unfulfilled. This kind of self-examination reflects how deeply emotional and traumatic infertility can be. Sometimes a couple may even keep the situation secretive to avoid embarrassing themselves in front of family and/or friends.

Sadly, this response only serves to heighten the pain that many couples experiencing infertility feel. Fifteen percent of couples in the United States cannot have children after one year of sexual relations. As a result, clinics specializing in aiding the reproductive process have sprung up all over the country. Couples spend many thousands of dollars to increase their *chances* of having a child.

There are several reproductive technologies which are currently in use, including fertility drugs, artificial insemination, in vitro fertilization (IVF), use of a surrogate mother, gamete intrafallopian transfer (GIFT), zygote intrafallopian transfer (ZIFT), and intracytoplasmic sperm injection (ICSI). Although these technologies are all different from each other, they all raise certain ethical issues which should concern anyone considering them. The issues as developed here should be nuanced by the fuller explanations in the book *Sexuality and Reproductive Technology* available from The Center for Bioethics and Human Dignity (see appendix).

A crucial issue in reproductive technologies is the safety of the embryos whether they are inside of a mother's body or in a laboratory. Because human life begins at conception, all embryos should be treated with the utmost care. For example:

Reprinted from Daniel McConchie, "Reproductive Technologies Overview," at www.bioethix.org/overviews/repover.html, by permission of the author.

1) A couple using IVF should decide ahead of time how many embryos to implant and attempt to create only that number of embryos. If more than the ideal number of embryos are created, the extras may be implanted with the others or frozen (to be implanted later)—whichever option poses less risk to the lives of the mother and embryos. No embryos should ever be discarded.

2) Only a limited number of embryos should be implanted following in vitro fertilization. Such an approach will decrease the chance that too many embryos will implant, thereby risking the lives of all the embryos and/or the mother.

> *"Selective reduction (abortion of some implanted, developing embryos so the others have a better chance to survive) is not an ethical option."*

3) A couple considering fertility drugs should research the options carefully. Some drugs may cause multiple eggs to mature rather than merely putting the body back into a normal, healthy, fertile state. Potentially harmful multiple pregnancies can result. One drug, clomiphene citrate, does not carry the risk of multiple pregnancies that some of the other fertility drugs now available do. Also, the multiple pregnancy risk can be minimized with the use of ultrasound to monitor the maturing egg(s). With monitoring, multiple pregnancies can be avoided.

4) Selective reduction (abortion of some implanted, developing embryos so the others have a better chance to survive) is not an ethical option. However, selective reduction should not be necessary if an appropriate number of embryos are implanted in the first place.

5) A couple should only consider implantation procedures whose percentage of success is equal to or greater than that of unassisted natural implantation. Otherwise, embryos are being placed at greater risk than is normally the case in human reproduction.

Ethical Problems Abound When Children Have More Than Two Parents

It is not advisable to use donor eggs and/or sperm in any reproductive technologies for a variety of reasons:

1) Who are the parents? Are they the ones whose genetic material (sperm and egg) combine to form the child or the people who raise the child? This question *might* be a simple one for the parents caring for the child, but how simple is that question from the viewpoint of the child? Sometimes, legal battles even result between the sets of parents involved in one child's life.

2) Should children know that one or both of his or her (rearing) parents did not provide the egg or sperm which brought them into being? Should children have access to the donor(s) (genetic parents)? Should genetic parents have visitation rights?

3) A distinctive imbalance may be introduced into a marriage where donor

eggs or sperm are used in place of one parent's eggs or sperm. There is the possibility of resentment from the partner whose eggs or sperm were not used. ("You take care of her! She's your child.") Accusations of unfaithfulness can result because, in a real, genetic sense, one of the spouses has had a child with another person. Emotional attachment to the "mystery person" can also develop in the spouse who genetically had the child with the donor.

4) These and other difficulties flow from violating the "one flesh" model of marriage in Scripture, in which children are literally to be the result of the two married parents (and their eggs and sperm) becoming "one flesh."

Surrogate Motherhood Should Be Generally Avoided

The most common form of surrogacy involves inseminating the surrogate with the husband's sperm—generally because the wife cannot carry a child through pregnancy. Such an arrangement should be avoided because a donor egg is involved, as explained above. Even when a donor egg is not involved—e.g., when the husband's sperm and wife's egg are joined *in vitro*—the bonding problems discussed below generally make such an agreement unwise. Particularly problematic are commercial arrangements in which surrogates receive payment for producing a child beyond expenses they incur. Like the selling of organs, such arrangements wrongly commercialize the body. In fact, financial contracts essentially entail the purchasing of the baby and imply an unacceptable form of ownership of human beings. Less problematic are altruistic surrogacies such as rescue surrogacies where a woman acts to save an embryo that would otherwise be destroyed.

Whenever donor eggs/sperm or a surrogate are used, the question of bonding can affect all parties involved. Bonds can develop between child and genetic parent(s), between surrogate mother and child, and between the genetic parents. The risk that inappropriate bonds will be created through the reproductive process is very real and can cause many problems. On many occasions, surrogate mothers have sued the genetic parents for custody after the baby was born or for the right to abort a malformed fetus even though the genetic parents wanted the child to live.

> *"One serious consideration should be the prudence of seeking to have a child with reproductive technologies when the costs and/or risks are so great."*

Alternatives to Reproductive Technologies Should Be Considered

One serious consideration should be the prudence of seeking to have a child with reproductive technologies when the costs and/or risks are so great. There are two primary concerns:

1) The money could go towards meeting another great need. It can be difficult to imagine anything more important than the creation of life. However, we also

have a responsibility to be concerned about those people already in the world today. There are people in many parts of the world without adequate medical care. For example, it costs just pennies per person to inoculate them against many of the world's greatest killers.

2) Adopting a child is often an option for people to consider. It's true that it is difficult to adopt in some countries, but international adoption is gaining popularity because of the number of orphaned children and speed with which the adoption process can often be completed. There are many children in the world in need of a home. In Cambodia, many children have been orphaned through years of war. In China where the government allows parents to have only one child, many female babies are left with orphanages by parents who want a boy. In Bulgaria, a reported average of 90% of the many children in orphanages will become criminals unless they are adopted. Those who are able should investigate the possibility of international adoption before ruling it out.

Caution Is Warranted

Undergoing reproductive treatments is very costly. *In vitro* fertilization costs between $10,000 and $20,000. Surrogacy can cost between $20,000 and $40,000. And these treatments do not guarantee that a child will result. In fact, clinics average only 20–40% live birth success rates. However, these success rates are most likely this high due to the implantation of multiple embryos and selective abortion which is very problematic ethically. Following ethical guidelines that protect human life from conception would probably make the percentage much lower.

Many people experience a very natural urge to be parents. Some are seeking to satisfy this urge using reproductive technologies without fully understanding all their implications. Before using technological methods of reproduction, it is wise to study in-depth the available options, understand the ethical issues involved, and above all, seek the will of God before moving ahead.

Multiple Births Are a Harmful Consequence of Assisted Reproduction

by Ezekiel J. Emanuel

About the author: *Ezekiel J. Emanuel is chairman of the department of clinical ethics at the National Institutes of Health.*

Just like the McCaughey septuplets of Iowa, whose first birthday [on November 26, 1998] recently made headlines in *People* magazine, the Chukwu octuplets of Texas [born in December 1998] have become a media spectacle. Daily bulletins detailing each child's respiratory status, ultrasound results, and other developments fill the papers—not just the tabloids, but respectable outlets like the *New York Times* and the *Washington Post*, as well. Inevitably, writers describe the eight live births in glowing terms—amazing, wonderful, even a miracle; they describe the mother as the brave survivor of adversity; they portray the hard-battling physicians as heroes and champions.

But what are we all celebrating? Modern reproductive technologies have brought the miracle of children to many infertile couples, thereby producing enormous good. The McCaughey septuplets and Chukwu octuplets, however, represent too much of that good thing. They are the product of fertility technology misused—an error, not a wonder, and one that even the few public voices of skepticism seem not fully to appreciate.

Medical Problems Associated with Multiple Pregnancies

First and most obvious, large multiple births lead to all sorts of medical problems, for mothers and children alike. Nkem Chukwu had to stay in the hospital for months prior to delivery, on a bed that tilted her nearly upside down. It's too early to know how well her surviving children will fare (one died seven days after birth), but the odds do not favor them. Among children born prematurely and weighing just two pounds or less—the largest of the Chukwu infants

Reprinted from Ezekiel J. Emanuel, "Eight Is Too Many," *The New Republic*, January 25, 1999, by permission of *The New Republic*; ©1999, The New Republic, Inc.

weighed one pound, eleven ounces at birth—breathing difficulties, brain dam-age, and fluid imbalances are not rare.

The result is a comparatively high level of infant mortality and, in the sur-vivors, long-term complications. Studies of low-birth-weight children (not from multi-fetal pregnancies but from pre-mature births) have shown that ap-proximately 20 percent have severe disabilities; among those weighing less than 750 grams (1.7 pounds) at birth, 50 percent have functional im-pairments. A recent study that fol-lowed these very small infants to school showed that up to 50 percent of them scored low on standardized intelligence tests, including 21 percent who were mentally retarded. In addition, nine percent had cerebral palsy, and 25 percent had severe vision problems. As a result, 45 percent ended up enrolling in special-education programs.

> *"The real way to assess these miraculous pregnancies—indeed, any pregnancy—is whether they are ultimately good for children. Quite clearly, they are not."*

Equally important, but rarely articulated, are the emotional health risks chil-dren in multiple births face. Loving and raising children through the normal de-velopmental milestones is enormously wonderful and rewarding. But it is also hard work. Raising children is not a sprint to a healthy birth but a marathon through variable terrain until the goal of independent adulthood. The real way to assess these miraculous pregnancies—indeed, any pregnancy—is whether they are ultimately good for children. Quite clearly, they are not.

The Demands of Raising So Many Children

Attending to the physical, emotional, intellectual, and social needs of children for 18 years is hard and demanding. For infants and toddlers there are the sim-ple physical demands—feeding, changing diapers, bathing, chasing after them to prevent injuries. Then there are the emotional and intellectual demands—cuddling them, talking to them, responding meaningfully to their smiles and first words, reading books to them, playing with them and their toys, handling the tantrums, and so on. And, while the physical demands may lessen once chil-dren grow (although parents who often feel like chefs, maids, chauffeurs, and all-around gofers may disagree with that), the emotional and intellectual de-mands become more complex with time. Older children need help with home-work, mediation of sibling rivalry, constructive discipline, support in the trials and tribulations of friendships, encouragement in their participation in sports and other activities, help in coping with losses and defeats, and guidance through the many pitfalls of adolescence.

It is challenging enough to balance the demands of one or two children of dif-ferent ages and attend to their needs; it is simply not physically possible for two parents to do this successfully for seven children of the same age, even if one of the parents is a full-time caregiver. Regardless of the motivation, dedication, love, or stamina of these parents, the sheer limitations of time make it impossible for each of seven identically aged children to receive appropriate parental attention and affection.

Just ask yourself: Would you trade being born a healthy single or twin for being born one of the "miraculous" septuplets, even a healthy one? Most of us would probably say "no" because of parental attention we would have lost. And we would be right to think that way.

Caregivers Cannot Substitute for Parents

The McCaugheys' experience proves the point. They have been able to raise their septuplets for one year only because they can fall back on a veritable army of volunteers—scores of people with tightly coordinated schedules who assist in the food preparation, feeding, diapering, and care of the seven babies. Few families with quintuplets or more children can expect or rely on such community effort. (Indeed, a Washington, D.C., couple who bore quintuplets had hardly any community help at all until some belated publicity highlighted the family's plight.) And, while the McCaugheys' community-wide effort appears to have worked for the first year of life, it's hardly a sure thing that the assistance will always be there. The first is the year when, despite the demands on time, parents are most interchangeable and caregiving has the greatest, most unmitigated emotional rewards. The terrible twos and threes will try the patience and dedication of volunteers.

> *"[The McCaugheys] have been able to raise their septuplets for one year only because they can fall back on a veritable army of volunteers."*

What's more, having multiple caregivers cannot fully substitute for parental time. While it's true that many children do just fine spending large amounts of time in paid day care, where multiple providers care for them, these children at least have the chance to go home and have one-on-one parental time spread among just a few siblings, of different ages. (Having multiple caregivers also becomes more problematic as the children grow, because of child-rearing styles that may differ from those of the parents, particularly on issues like discipline.) This is not possible in the McCaughey or Chukwu families, and it never will be. Spending just 20 minutes a day focusing on each individual child—hardly a lavish amount—will take nearly two and a half hours each day. When competing with sleep, meals, shopping, and all the other demands of basic existence for a family with septuplets, this focused time is likely to disappear.

The Financial Costs

Remember, too, that, while the McCaughey septuplets seem to have brought together a community to support their care, such children also impose significant costs on the community. It is now estimated that the hospital costs from birth to discharge (or death) for the Chukwu infants will exceed $2 million. And the health care costs don't stop after birth. Any complications—neurological, vision, or other problems—can drive the medical care costs sky-high. Plus, no one knows how much will be required for permanent problems that require ongoing special-education and other accommodations. Yes, there's health insurance. But health insurance exists to cover ill health and problems such as cancer, genetic defects, and accidents that are the result of random chance. The birth of octuplets, by contrast, is not a chance event; it is the result of deliberate actions (or inactions) by physicians, patients, and society. Remember, too, that financial resources are limited; money spent on octuplets is money not spent on other children with special health care and educational needs.

Preventing Multiple Births

For these reasons, the standard of medical care is not to proceed with such large multiple births. But this raises legitimate ethical problems for many couples. The most common method for interrupting multiple pregnancies is "selective reduction"—that is, doctors abort some of the fetuses for the sake of the mother's health. Many people believe couples who agree to infertility treatments must not only be informed about—but should consent to—the potential need for selective reduction even before beginning the treatments. Yet this is clearly not an option for families like the McCaugheys and the Chukwus, who oppose abortion on religious grounds.

Fortunately, this issue doesn't have to be so morally knotty. In the usual treatment for problems with egg maturation and release (this is what both the McCaughey and Chukwu families were treated for), doctors prescribe drugs such as human menopausal gonadotropin (hMG) or Clomiphene (commonly known as Clomid) to stimulate egg development. Then they administer an additional drug, human chorionic gonadatropin (hCG), to induce ovulation. Using measurements of estrogen and ultrasound monitoring, physicians can assess the number of egg follicles developing in the ovaries. If they observe too many developing follicles, making the likelihood of multiple fertilizations high, physicians can withhold the drugs necessary to stimulate ovulation and advise against intercourse or withhold sperm injection until the next

"The media must stop glorifying the septuplets and octuplets."

cycle, when they can go through the process again. To be sure, that treatment process can be a little more frustrating for aspiring parents. And many couples are reluctant to skip a cycle because it wastes thousands of dollars on the drugs and treatments, usually out of their own pockets. But carrying septuplets to term has costs, too.

In the end, new laws or regulations won't fix this problem. The real solution is leadership by the medical profession and by the media. Reproductive specialists who care for infertile couples are not simply passive technicians following the orders of the parents. They are engaged professionals guiding important technology that can create great joy—but also great pain. Professionalism requires deliberating with the parents about the goals and purposes of the treatments; doctors should draw upon their experience to advise and strongly recommend the best course to the parents, which is to avoid large multiple pregnancies.

More Is Not Necessarily Better

And the media must stop glorifying the septuplets and octuplets. We live in an era that measures success in terms of quantity, that thinks bigger is necessarily better, where the best is defined by size. The best movie is the one that makes the most money; the best law firm is the one with the highest billings; the best painting is auctioned for the highest price; and the best book is the best-selling book. But, in this case, bigger may not be better—indeed, it may actually be worse. The true miracle of birth is the mysterious process by which the fusing of an egg and a sperm can create in just nine months the complex organism that is an infant with the potential to become an independent, thinking, feeling, socially responsible adult. In this way, the millions of babies born each year are miraculous whether born of singleton, twin, triplet, or octuplet pregnancies. It is the wonder of each infant that we should celebrate.

Cloning Is Not an Acceptable Means of Reproduction

by *Commonweal*

About the author: Commonweal *is an independent journal of opinion edited and managed by lay Catholics.*

From Scotland comes news that a team of fearless scientists has cloned a sheep. One might consider this development one worrisome step for sheep, but more likely it is a very big and very dangerous step for humankind.

The Uproar over Dolly

"Dolly," as she was christened, was produced in a laboratory where a cell taken from the udder of one sheep was fused with another sheep's egg, from which the nucleus had been removed. The resulting embryo was then implanted in a surrogate mother and brought to term. Dolly is the genetic twin of the sheep from whom the cell was first taken, and her arrival promises benefits in scientific knowledge, agriculture, and medicine.

Dolly caused an uproar in large part because, though theoretically possible, it had long proved technically unfeasible to clone mammals. It is now expected that it is only a matter of time before someone succeeds in cloning the most successful mammal of all—namely, humans. At this point in the conquest of nature by science, it is important to reassert that not everything that can be done should be done. Even Ian Wilmut, the scientist chiefly responsible for bringing Dolly into the world, considers the idea of cloning human beings "offensive . . . , ethically unacceptable." His instincts are sound. However, a critical observer might also ask why someone opposed to the likely uses of this technology nevertheless decided to set us off on this path.

Some embrace the prospect of manufacturing human life in laboratories. Such thinking seems more a confirmation of the modern trivialization of the meaning of sex than any sober assessment of what is at stake when technology plays so large a part in human reproduction. The Catholic position on these questions is clear-cut—perhaps too clear-cut. Because it draws the line on intervention in procreation at contraception, the church's often astute warnings about the dehumanizing of sex and reproduction have fallen on deaf ears. That's unfortunate, because the human values the church rightly defends in questioning advanced reproductive technologies make its hair-splitting over "barrier methods" and the so-called "contraceptive mentality" seem like mere intellectualized prudery. In reality, much more is at stake.

Reproductive Freedom Has Limits

There are sound moral reasons why human communities have always tied sexual desire to love, and love to marriage, and marriage to the care of children. Neither the extreme view demanding that every sexual act be "open" to procreation, nor the modern presumption that we should be free to desexualize and depersonalize the act of procreation, is the best way to promote human flourishing. But where to draw the line along the continuum of interventions is difficult. In the acceptance of each new technology—artificial insemination, *in vitro* fertilization, surrogate motherhood—a logic of justification is advanced that makes the next moral hurdle seem lower still. Yet as Dr. Wilmut's own trepidation attests, there is widespread uneasiness over giving scientists and potential DNA donors the ability to determine the entire genetic make-up of new human lives. Cloning, with the genetic manipulation and engineering it heralds, may be a line even many who champion "reproductive freedom" will not want to cross.

Still, it is argued that clones ought to be considered little more than "delayed twins." That is true, in a strictly genetic sense. Certainly identical twins occur in nature. But why should anyone be allowed to determine the *entire* genetic identity of another person? Granting such power over someone else's life— even the life of one's own offspring—is an unwarranted circumscribing of individuality and human possibility. We simply don't have the right to decide such things for others. Parents are entrusted with the lives of their children; they are not the owners or determiners of those lives. As Daniel Callahan has written, cloning "would be a profound threat to what might be called the right to our own identity."

Human cloning would play havoc with notions of parenthood, kinship,

> *"Infertility is not sufficient justification for any and all means of bringing a child into the world."*

the distinct dignity of children in regard to their parents, and perhaps even the sanctity of life. The possibilities for mischief seem endless, and endlessly dizzying. A woman could, for example, give birth to her own twin. As with justification for most reproductive technologies, the desire of an infertile couple for a genetic child may prove to be the most compelling reason for resorting to cloning. Infertility can be a terrible personal loss. Still, infertility is not sufficient justification for any and all means of bringing a child into the world. Cloning would represent yet a further commodification of procreation; in its asexual method of reproduction and the genetic asymmetry of the child produced, cloning further relativizes the most fundamental of human relationships: that of wife and husband and parents and children. Technological wizardry must not be allowed to undermine monogamous marriage and the biological family. Science and technology should serve the common good, not its own self-aggrandizing imperatives or mere individual desire.

An Inhuman Process

When it comes to cloning, we are a bit like a gardener who thinks she can manage the ecology of an entire forest. There is too much we do not know, too much we can never know. Worse, in almost every respect—from the discarding of "surplus" embryos to the possible creation of genetic monstrosities—cloning requires that we regard another human being as a means to an end, and not as an end in itself. Indeed, the very attempt to clone humans constitutes experimentation (it is not a medical procedure) on someone who is incapable of giving consent, a violation of the most fundamental principles of medicine and science. In sum, like abortion and euthanasia, cloning human beings moves us a step closer to an openly utilitarian definition of human dignity and life.

Justified in the name of scientific progress and humanitarian relief, cloning will be a powerful temptation. Yet the intuition that tells us there is something inherently inhuman in the laboratory production of human beings is sound. Science and technology enable us to transcend our physical limitations, but in doing so we run the risk at a certain point of betraying our true natures. In the creation of children it is important that we prize our full, embodied humanity, and not just one aspect of it. When it comes to separating reproduction from human sexuality, the siren call of scientific progress is largely a ruse. The kind of control over human life and destiny promised by these new reproductive technologies is far too potent to be left in the hands of scientists or anyone else. As our brave new world of self-creation unfolds, we must guard against progress in the name of humanity that in fact dehumanizes.

Chapter 4

What Ethics Should Guide Biomedical Research?

Stem Cell Research and Human Cloning: An Overview

by **Gregg Easterbrook**

About the author: *Gregg Easterbrook is a senior editor of the* National Review *and the author of* A Moment on the Earth: The Coming Age of Environmental Optimism.

For John Gearhart, a biologist at Johns Hopkins University, professional life had been an exercise in slamming against walls. Gearhart's specialty is Down's syndrome, triggered when one of the infant body's chromosomes copies itself once too often. Gearhart had spent 20 years trying to puzzle out this genetic error. "All our data suggested that Down's was caused by something that happens quite early in embryo genesis," he says—but the only way to find out what happens then would be to conduct experiments on human embryos, a prospect repugnant at best. Trying to think his way out of the problem, Gearhart wondered; What if there was a way to isolate and culture embryonic "stem cells," the precursors of all body parts? If they could be transferred to the laboratory, it might become possible to study the cytology of conception.

The Benefits of Stem-Cell Research

Stem cells are the philosopher's stones of biology, magical objects capable of metamorphosing into any component of the body: heart, nerves, blood, bone, muscle. Mammal embryos begin as a clump of stem cells that gradually subdivides into the specific functional parts of the organism. Researchers have long assumed that, because stem cells are genetically programmed to change into other things, it would never be possible to control them, let alone culture them. But Gearhart and another researcher working independently, James Thomson of the University of Wisconsin, found this is not so.

In November 1998, Gearhart and Thomson announced that they had each isolated embryonic stem cells and induced them to begin copying themselves without turning into anything else. In so doing, they apparently discovered a way to make stem cells by the billions, creating a biological feedstock that might, in turn, be employed to produce brand-new, healthy human tissue. That is, they discovered how to fabricate the stuff of which humanity is made.

Researchers had already demonstrated that stem cells might be a medical boon by showing that such tissues extracted from aborted fetuses

> *"If researchers can convert stem cells into regular cells . . . then physicians might cure Parkinson's, diabetes, leukemia, heart congestion, and many other maladies."*

could reverse symptoms of Parkinson's disease. But so many fetuses were required to treat just one patient that the technique could never be practical, to say nothing of its harrowing character. By contrast, Gearhart and Thomson have found that stem cells can be reproduced roughly in the way that pharmaceutical manufacturers make drugs.

If researchers can convert stem cells into regular cells like blood or heart muscle and then put them back into the body, then physicians might cure Parkinson's, diabetes, leukemia, heart congestion, and many other maladies, replacing failing cells with brand-new tissue. Costly afflictive procedures such as bone-marrow transplants might become easier and cheaper with the arrival of stem-cell-based "universal donor" tissue that does not provoke the immune-rejection response. The need for donor organs for heart or liver transplants might fade, as new body parts are cultured artificially. Ultimately, mastery of the stem cell might lead to practical, affordable ways to eliminate many genetic diseases through DNA engineering, while extending the human life span. Our near descendants might live in a world in which such killers as cystic fibrosis and sickle-cell anemia are one-in-a-million conditions, while additional decades of life are the norm.

Granted, sensational promises made for new medical technologies don't always come to pass, and some researchers are skeptical about whether stem-cell technology will pan out. But Harold Varmus, head of the National Institutes of Health (NIH), recently declared, "This research has the potential to revolutionize the practice of medicine." Notes John Fletcher, a bioethicist at the University of Virginia, "Soon every parent whose child has diabetes or any cell-failure disease is going to be riveted to this research, because it's the answer." Ron McKay, a stem-cell researcher at the National Institute of Neurological Disorders and Stroke, says, "We are now at the center of biology itself." Simply put, the control of human stem cells may open the door to the greatest medical discovery since antibiotics.

But there are disquieting aspects to stem-cell research, too. The first is that, for now, the only way to start the process of controlled stem-cell duplication is to extract samples from early human life. Gearhart used fetuses aborted by Baltimore women; Thomson, embryos no longer wanted by Wisconsin in vitro fertilization (IVF) clinics. Gearhart, Thomson, and other stem-cell researchers propose to continue drawing on such "resources," as some bloodless medical documents refer to the fetus and the embryo. This is possible because, even though Congress has placed a moratorium on federal funding for experimentation on most IVF embryos and most kinds of fetal tissue, no law governs what scientists can do to incipient life using private funding, either in research settings or within the burgeoning IVF industry.

Because the rules have banned embryo research by federally funded biologists, but not comparable private science, Congress has created the preposterous situation in which most stem-cell research is not being done by publicly funded scientists who must pass multiple levels of peer review and disclose practically everything about their work. Instead, most stem-cell science is in the hands of corporate-backed researchers. Gearhart's and Thomson's projects, for example, are being underwritten by Geron, a company whose name derives from "gerontology," and which anticipates a licensing El Dorado if stem-cell-based good health can be patented and sold to the seniors' market. "That a sensitive category of research is legal for people who are not publicly accountable, but illegal for those who are accountable, is just very strange," says Thomson.

> *"The greatest anxiety about stem-cell research is that it will make human cloning respectable."*

But the greatest anxiety about stem-cell research is that it will make human cloning respectable. Many of the techniques being perfected for the medical application of stem cells are just a hop, skip, and a jump away from those that could apply to reproductive cloning. Society isn't even close to thinking through the legal, ethical, regulatory, and religious implications, but, thanks to stem-cell research, cloning may arrive much, much sooner than anyone expects.

Stem Cells Are Undifferentiated Cells

Stem cells stand in the vanguard of human life. When a sperm penetrates an egg, it triggers a majestic sequence whose first step is to create a new structure that is composed mainly of stem cells. Biologists call such cells "undifferentiated," meaning they have not yet decided what they will be. Once the fertilized ovum implants in the uterus, differentiation starts. Some stem cells become placenta; others begin differentiating into the baby's organs, tissue, or blood. A stem cell might divide into any of the many components of the body, but, once it does, it can only continue growing as that part.

Because once a stem cell begins to differentiate it cannot turn back, biologists assumed that all stem cells could never turn back. But, in 1981, experimenters succeeded in extracting stem cells from the embryos of mice. By the mid-'90s, researchers had learned which chemicals instruct mouse stem cells to become particular tissue types and how to insert the new tissues back into mice. Loren Field of Indiana University became so adept at signaling mouse stem cells to become mouse heart cells that "his lab is almost pulsating with heart cells beating in dishes," Gearhart says.

> *"If it's okay to terminate a fetus, why isn't it okay to experiment on the remains?"*

But, though the stem cell clearly dominates human germination, mysteries abound. The overriding enigma is why stem cells work so phenomenally well in the womb but then stop working when the body matures. After all, every cell in the body contains a complete DNA blueprint for a person's being. In theory, if your coronary arteries became clogged, your DNA could direct the creation of stem cells that would subdivide into new arteries to replace the failing tissue. In some lower animals that regrow limbs, this is roughly what happens. But, after reaching maturity, the human body never again draws on its DNA blueprints to replace tissue more complex than skin. Thomas Okarma, vice president for research for Geron, asks, "Who is really more highly evolved, the lizard that can grow new body parts, or us?" Using stem cells to make fresh new tissue or organs, as if the body was still nascent, is the revolutionary therapy Geron hopes to market. . . .

Unease over Obtaining Stem Cells from Human Embryos

More pressing is resolving the basic ethics of stem-cell research. When Gearhart first proposed to use aborted fetuses as the basis of his stem-cell research, his sponsoring university was not thrilled. Although research on aborted fetuses is legal, it's a gray area, and restrictions are many. Occasionally, a maverick researcher protests this situation by asking the discomfiting post-Roe question: If it's okay to terminate a fetus, why isn't it okay to experiment on the remains? Few object to research on the cadavers of adults. Do we ban research on the aborted out of a sense of guilt that we should not add mutilation to the wrongs suffered by a life denied?

Gearhart's stem-cell extractions employ "fetal tissue," which researchers may view as differing from fetuses, though the reasoning is obscure. Johns Hopkins put his proposal through eleven levels of legal and ethical review, and also review by the university's security office, which worried that the degenerate fringe of the pro-life movement would target the project. Gearhart chose to focus on a type of stem cell called a "primordial germ cell," which he extracts from a region on the aborted fetus called the "urogenital ridge." Gearhart will work with fetuses no more than nine weeks old. Around nine weeks is when the fetus begins to appear recognizably human, though it is believed there is no consciousness until weeks later. He says, and not without defensiveness, "Remember, it's not criminal at this point." Technically, Gearhart's project might have qualified for federal funding, but he never asked, knowing there would be an outcry.

For his part, Thomson isolates stem cells from the "inner mass" of roughly week-old embryos that were conceived in IVF clinics but which couples elected not to use. Thomson thus extracts tissue from the early, pre-uterus stage in which it is impossible to tell which stem cells will become the placenta and which the person. Strictly speaking, then, Thomson has no way of knowing whether the cells he plucks could have grown or would have been lost anyway. Though Thomson's extractions are timed to occur at what seemed to him the least ethically perilous moment of incipient life, in the cockeyed world of bioethics regulation, his recent experiments clearly could not have qualified for federal funding, since he was employing embryos.

Both Gearhart and Thomson call on Congress to enact clear legal guidelines for their field. Thomson says, "The human embryo is the most special cell in biology, and there are just some things you shouldn't do to embryos"—mainly clone them. The primary point stem-cell researchers make in their own favor is that the cells they experiment upon, once brought into the lab, might be made into muscle or blood, but can no longer become a human being. This assertion seems true, though slightly cute, since the reason the cells cease being capable of personhood is that they've been artificially snatched from it. But then no one plans to conceive the IVF embryos that Thomson gets, and the fetuses Gearhart receives have already had their lives terminated. Neither biologist can change these things, though both might change others' lives for the better. . . .

The Need for Public Debate

Bringing public funding to stem-cell research will force a public debate on this new biology. There has been little so far. In Congress, a few members, such as Representative Jay Dickey of Arkansas, have declared themselves opposed, for pro-life reasons, to any research on embryonic cells. A few members, such as Senator Tom Harkin of Iowa, have openly endorsed stem-cell studies. Senator Arlen Specter of Pennsylvania was expected this year to introduce legislation making human stem-cell research explicitly legal, as it is in the United Kingdom. But Specter now says he will postpone action, feeling the time isn't right.

Many researchers were pleased by this decision, fearing that drawing public attention to today's stem-cell research might only provoke a backlash, whereas, once treatments derived from stem cells are available, lobbying impetus for the technology will be unstoppable. But, while the science world may be trusted to police its own for professionalism and high standards, it can't

> *"While the science world may be trusted to police its own for professionalism and high standards, it can't be trusted with the ethical end of this debate."*

137

be trusted with the ethical end of this debate.

Science types tend to be unreflective boosters of funding, funding, and more funding. A 1994 NIH commission on whether to allow embryonic research endorsed it without meaningful objection, tossing off slighting remarks—like a statement that the human embryo is "significantly smaller than the period at the end of this sentence," as if that had anything to do with anything. Stem-cell research came over the horizon so fast that the 1994 panel's work quickly became obsolete, and now a National Bioethics Advisory Commission has been convened to study the latest developments. But it, too, seems mainly concerned with rationalizing the status quo. In January 1999, I watched as the bioethics commissioners had a chance to grill Gearhart and Thomson. The commissioners were awestruck and deferential, asking what they could do to help win stem-cell funding—not much more aggressively than Dolly the cloned sheep herself might have. Toward the end, one commissioner, Rhetaugh Dumas of the University of Michigan, asked the sole unfriendly question: Does stem-cell research have any downsides? When neither of the scientists spoke, Dumas looked around at her fellow commissioners and asked skittishly, "Was that an inappropriate question?" It wasn't a reassuring moment.

> *"Whether stem-cell research is ethically good, bad, or indifferent depends largely on when life begins."*

Controversy over When Life Begins

One reason the interplay between science and religion has become a topic again is that thoughtful researchers know biotechnology is raising questions science can't answer. For one, whether stem-cell research is ethically good, bad, or indifferent depends largely on when life begins, and on this subject there is neither definitive science nor ethics. Many Catholic, evangelical, and Islamic theorists say that life begins at the moment sperm meets egg; therefore, a single cell can have sacred rights. But this seems not quite right, because DNA sets from egg and sperm do not immediately merge; the ovum divides once before the onset of genetic recombination. Besides, what would happen if cloning rendered every cell in the body a potential person? Varmus, the NIH director, has asked, "If we say any cell has the potential to be a human being, then every time you cut your finger, do you have to wear black?"

Obstetricians sometimes mark the big moment as the time, around two weeks after conception, when the fertilized egg implants in the womb and pregnancy begins. Thomas Aquinas taught that the fetus became "ensouled" after about six weeks. This view, which was Vatican policy until 1869, differs only somewhat from Gearhart's conclusion that fetal tissue extractions should stop after about nine weeks. *Roe v. Wade* declared that the rights of life are in view when the fetus is capable of existing outside the mother, a milestone technology keeps pushing back toward the second trimester. Surely once brain activity begins, around the twenty-fifth week, the fetus has become human, leaving the late-term abortion a cause for moral abhorrence, except when the life of the mother is threatened. But, before that point, it's all speculation. . . .

Because the moral status of the early embryo is, at best, ambiguous, it seems likely society will decide that the first claim lies with those already alive, and permit further experimentation to generate stem cells. "We should respect every embryo," the bioethicist Caplan says, "but I'm not going to look at a person in a wheelchair and say, 'Sorry, you have to stay in that wheelchair for the rest of your life because of my belief that the frozen embryos in my liquid nitrogen might have become life.'" Thomson contends that stem-cell research is simply inevitable: "Even if we force it out of the United States and the European Union, it will still happen." Stem-cell medicine is coming, ready or not.

Can Stem Cells Be Obtained from Adults?

There is one possible avenue of escape from the moral enigmas of this research: if stem cells can be found in adults, there will be no need to draw on embryonic "resources." Biology textbooks call this quest hopeless, since by adulthood every cell is differentiated and incapable of further transformation. At least that was the view until February 1997, when the British researcher Ian Wilmut cloned Dolly. Essentially, he did this by taking cells from an adult lamb, making them act like stem cells, and then fusing their DNA into a donor egg which germinated into a baby lamb genetically identical to the adult. Mainstream biologists had thought that embryos, still rich in stem cells, might be cloned, but never adults—or that, if adult stem cells could be found, they would be incapable of reactivating. Since Dolly, however, cows and mice have been cloned from adult cells by variations on the Wilmut technique. Researchers are now finding indications that small amounts of stem cells continue to exist, overlooked, in the adult's nerve tissue and elsewhere; it may be that there are small adult stem-cell deposits throughout the body. . . .

Stem cells derived from adults would not only resolve qualms about embryonic tissue; they might have superior therapeutic properties. Suppose you had a liver disease. If one of your own cells could be used as the template for fresh stem cells that would then be converted into liver tissue, what would end up transplanted into you would contain your own DNA and antigens, which presumably would forestall tissue rejection. Transplants might

"If stem-cell research succeeds, the barriers against gene therapy may fall."

become something the typical person experienced several times in adulthood. Life expectancy would shoot upward, along with the health care share of GDP.

If any person's cells can be made into stem cells, gene therapy and gene engineering, hyped but so far very rare, might also become more common. For two decades, researchers such as W. French Anderson of the University of Southern California have labored to use genes to cure fatal childhood genetic conditions. It just hasn't worked. So far, the only way to deliver healthy DNA into patients is by using viral envelopes as little biological guided missiles. But the immune system shoots these missiles down, defeating the therapy. Anderson, a sainted physician who has spent most of his professional life seemingly inches shy of a great breakthrough, and who instead endlessly watched young patients die, has grown so frustrated he recently proposed attempting gene therapy within the womb. "Once the child is older, the cells may just be too developed to accept new genes," Anderson says—"older" in this sense meaning anyone who's been born.

In 1995, an NIH study panel called genetic therapy "a logical and natural progression in the application of fundamental biomedical science," which is certainly an engaging use of the term "natural." But there's no reason in principle to fear genetic theory, which simply represents using brainpower against medical problems that either God or evolution left for us to solve. And, if stem-cell research succeeds, the barriers against gene therapy may fall. Stem-cell based genetic therapy agents would contain the patient's own DNA code, with only the defective gene altered; the delivery vector would be not viruses but stem cells, which are designed to multiply like mad anyway. At the current rate of progress in research, stem-cell based gene therapy may not be far off, bringing cures to people now classified as incurable.

From Genetic Therapy to Genetic Engineering

And once you're standing on this hill, it's pretty easy to see over to the next peak: genetic engineering. Technically, genetic therapy would be a form of genetic engineering—the purpose would be to engineer out the recessive gene that causes cystic fibrosis or sickle-cell anemia, replacing it with healthy DNA that does not. Yet the same technology that may make this gene manipulation possible might make possible the substitution of new genes for DNA that isn't diseased. "DNA engineering itself is now straightforward," says Austin Smith, a biologist at the University of Edinburgh, though only for plants and mice. Plant breeders have been recombining DNA for a decade now, famously inserting fish genes into tomatoes so that they resist frost better, while many of the specialized types of mice used in lab experiments have engineered traits.

Though no gene engineering has been attempted on humans, there appear to be no special technical barriers against doing so. Silver, the Princeton biologist, argues that our generation will be looked back on as "the point in history when human beings gained the power to seize control of their own evolutionary destiny." Control over evolution might turn out well or badly, but there's no reason to reject it out of hand, since evolution has left humanity disease-prone, short-lived, and fragile. Why shouldn't we try to change that?

The disturbing question is whether we will begin sooner than we think through the consequences. Currently, NIH protocols—but not legislation—ban any attempt to alter the human "germline," meaning to change genes in a way that would be passed along to offspring. Gene therapy attempts have been confined to "somatic" cells, the nonreproductive parts of the body, with anything else considered taboo. Yet, in 1998, Louise Markert of the Duke University Medical Center asked the Recombinant DNA Advisory Committee, which supervises genetic experiments, to begin a debate on whether engineering of reproductive cells should be tested. It's not even the twenty-first century yet, and already earnest, respectable researchers are talking about altering human heredity. . . .

Stem-Cell Research and Human Cloning

Promising as stem-cell research is, what it's doing in the larger scheme is accumulating the technical information that will make human cloning possible. In principle, stem-cell technology might allow a clinic to isolate an adult's gene endowment, engineer it for frost resistance or God knows what else, and then, by allowing the new stem cells to reproduce themselves before implantation, clone unlimited facsimiles of the person.

It may be that the knowledge of cloning is unstoppable, in the sense that no force has ever incarcerated knowledge. And cloning should not be feared in and of itself, for there are arguments in its favor. Clones would be facsimiles of their parents (technically, parent) only in the physical sense. They'd be born as babies—no imaginable technology would create life directly as adults, making the business about rich men or dictators xeroxing themselves a Hollywood silliness that detracts from the serious arguments against cloning. Character-shaping effects of each generation's particular upbringing would inevitably make the cloned child differ from the parent, while a clone's thoughts, personality, and experiences would reflect the unique human dignity possessed by every individual. No one argues that each member of a pair of identical twins, who are genetic duplicates, does not possess unique dignity. . . .

Today's situation with stem cells and cloning might be likened to what would happen if a fleet of modern jet fighters were teleported back in time to ancient Sumeria. First, the ancients would marvel at the objects, noting their extraordinary complexity—as scientists marveled when they first glimpsed the extent of the double helix. Initially, they'd be too scared to touch, and some would argue that the gods would punish those who touched. Eventually, the fear would wane, and, by poking and prodding and pushing buttons, someone would

> *"It may be that the knowledge of cloning is unstoppable, in the sense that no force has ever incarcerated knowledge."*

manage to start one of the plane's engines, generating thunder and fire. At that point, the ancients would believe they had "discovered" the true purpose of the mysterious objects, and that, now being able to manipulate the planes, they had become masters of them.

141

Owing to the stem-cell breakthrough, there now stands the prospect that our children will not only live healthier lives but that their children will be the final generation of Homo sapiens, supplanted by Homo geneticus or whatever comes next. Homo erectus didn't last, so there's no reason to assume Homo sapiens won't ever give way to a next stage. If all goes well, the advent of control over our own cells might offer our grandchildren many things we would wish for them.

But it's all happening much, much faster than society understands. It's also happening under conditions in which we are telling ourselves that we understand genes because we have learned to make them do certain things, but we probably know little more about the totality of our DNA than would the ancient who doesn't even realize that airplanes are supposed to fly. It's time to move biotechnology to the center of the national debate, so that we can sort out its rights and wrongs before sheer technological momentum imposes an outcome upon us.

Research on Human Embryos Is Unethical

by John J. Miller

About the author: *John J. Miller is national political reporter for the* National Review, *a biweekly journal of conservative opinion.*

Senator Tom Harkin wanted to sound sophisticated at a hearing on the complicated subject of embryonic-cell research in December 1998. "It is my belief and my opinion, based upon a lot of study of this, that [stem cells] do not fall under the ban on human-embryo research," declared the Iowa Democrat. Then he read the law aloud, including the part that defines embryos as organisms derived from human diploid cells. "I don't even know what that is," he announced.

A seventh-grade biology textbook might have come in handy. Diploid cells are those that contain complete sets of chromosome pairs. In other words, all cells are diploid cells except for eggs and sperm. But Harkin wasn't interested in the details. Neither were his scientific allies at the witness table. A powerful coalition including the Clinton administration and pro-abortion groups, as well as biotechnology companies, universities, and patient-advocacy outfits, are determined to railroad right-to-lifers on an emerging and bitterly contested moral issue.

Saving Some Lives by Destroying Others

The stakes for both sides are high. With the partial-birth-abortion fight essentially lost—Congress remains unable to override a presidential veto, the initiative process hasn't worked, and the courts have repeatedly struck down state laws banning the practice—pro-lifers now identify embryo research as a top legislative priority. But they are pitted against interests that stand to win millions of dollars in federal funding—and potentially make many millions more if firms bring products based on this research to the marketplace.

The debate slipped into overdrive in November 1998, when scientists announced that they had isolated human embryonic stem cells, primitive cells that, like the stem of a plant, can grow into any part of the human body. Adults carry stem cells, but they are not as versatile as the ones found in embryos. If nudged the right way, embryonic stem cells can grow into a wide variety of healthy tissues and organs, which can then be transplanted into people suffering from Alzheimer's disease, diabetes, heart conditions—anything in which degenerative cells play a role.

Clinical applications are still years away, but stem-cell research holds almost limitless promise. Lifespans could increase by decades. William Haseltine, head of Human Genome Sciences, a private firm in Maryland, even told the *Washington Post*, "This

> *"Stem-cell research holds almost limitless promise.... There's only one problem: Embryonic-stem-cell research kills living embryos."*

is the first time we can conceive human immortality." There's only one problem: Embryonic-stem-cell research kills living embryos. John Gearhart of Johns Hopkins University performed experiments on aborted fetuses seven to nine weeks old. The University of Wisconsin's James Thomson obtained unwanted embryos from in vitro fertilization banks. He destroyed 36 of them to produce five cultures of living tissue. Michael West of Advanced Cell Technology, a Massachusetts company, harvested stem cells by creating and then killing embryos.

Violating the Federal Ban on Destructive Embryo Research

Federal dollars didn't pay for their work. In 1996, Congress banned funding for destructive embryo research. But shortly after Gearhart, Thomson, and West went public, the push began to circumvent the law. Senator Arlen Specter of Pennsylvania, who is pro-choice, convened a series of hearings to trumpet the findings. Scientists and biotechnology companies urged taxpayer support. The American Association of Medical Colleges rallied dozens of patients-rights groups, ranging from the American Lung Association to the National Osteoporosis Foundation.

Meanwhile, the Clinton administration went to work. The law is pretty clear: The federal government can't pay for killing human embryos. So supporters of the research got clever. What if somebody not funded by the government did the killing, and then sent the stem cells to researchers who take taxpayer dollars? In December 1998, Harold Varmus, director of the National Institutes of Health (NIH), asked for a legal opinion from the Department of Health and Human Services (HHS).

The department's lawyers reported back in a January 15, 1999, memo. Funding embryonic-stem-cell research is permissible because stem cells are not embryos, wrote general counsel Harriet S. Rabb, formerly a board member of the New York Civil Liberties Union. For her analysis, Rabb leaned on deputy counsel Marcy Wilder, who worked as a National Abortion and Reproductive Rights Action League lobbyist before joining HHS two years ago. The Rabb-Wilder memo essentially argued that NIH researchers can't actually kill the embryos—

at least not while they're on government time—but are allowed to work on embryo parts.

The legal logic isn't compelling, because the congressional ban is broad, forbidding funding for "research in which a human embryo or embryos are destroyed, discarded, or knowingly subjected to risk of injury or death." The moral logic doesn't make much sense either. "It's like saying you won't pay to have someone kill me, but will experiment on my heart right after watching someone else rip it out of my body," says Richard Doerflinger of the National Conference of Catholic Bishops. "Either way I'm dead." In February 1999, 70 House members and seven senators wrote to HHS secretary Donna Shalala to protest her lawyers' administrative nullification of federal law. Even Senator Specter sensed the HHS memo's weakness. "We are in very deep water," he admitted to the *New York Times*.

The Rabb-Wilder memo nevertheless provided enough cover. Varmus eagerly announced that NIH would begin funding the controversial research, and Shalala brushed off congressional objections. NIH is expected to issue research-application guidelines by summer 1999.

Embryo Research Destigmatizes Abortion

Abortion-rights advocates can't wait for NIH to turn on the funding spigot, because destructive embryo research destigmatizes abortion. Just imagine an abortion counselor telling a young woman that ending her pregnancy will help scientists improve another person's life. And pro-abortion advocates relish the sight of pro-lifers arguing against the Juvenile Diabetes Foundation. Biotechnology companies with short-term capitalization, meanwhile, are looking for quick returns on their investments, and government-sponsored stem-cell research aids them enormously. Because their work will create a caste of human embryos living and dying in labs for the purpose of tissue and organ donation, they also want the implied social seal of approval that government funding affords. Universities too are always eager for new sources of revenue.

Eventually advances in biotechnology could make embryonic research unnecessary. "There are no fundamental barriers to achieving pluripotent stem cells from adults," says John Fagan, a molecular biologist who heads Genetic ID, an Iowa-based company. In other words, stem cells harvested from adults may be reprogrammed in ways that give them the medical versatility of embryonic stem cells. On March 4, 1999, researchers at the Howard Hughes Medical Center in Pasadena, California, said that they had grown stem cells from living nerve tissue. And in January 1999, a team of Canadian and Italian scientists working on mice announced that they were able to transform

> *"Imagine an abortion counselor telling a young woman that ending her pregnancy will help scientists improve another person's life."*

neural stem cells into blood-making bone-marrow stem cells—a process that in theory should work in human beings.

But it will take a few years for these innovations to mature, and only a pro-life minority seems willing to wait. "These are very debatable issues," says Ronald Eastman, CEO of Geron, a California-based company that funded the Johns Hopkins and Wisconsin experiments. "But the benefits far outweigh the concerns." In December 1998, Arlen Specter wondered whether embryonic-stem-cell research would create "a realistic fountain of youth." His allies are ready to find out, even if it means bankrolling a culture of death.

Research on Human Embryos Can Be Ethical

by Arthur Caplan

About the author: *Arthur Caplan is director of the Center for Bioethics at the University of Pennsylvania and the author of numerous books on medical ethics, including* Moral Matters: Ethical Issues in Medicine and the Life Sciences.

Editor's note: In November 1998 the Department of Health and Human Services (HHS) announced that it was considering allowing the National Institutes of Health to fund research on human embryonic stem cells, which are derived from aborted embryos or embryos created through in vitro fertilization. This viewpoint was given as testimony in a December 1998 Senate hearing in which experts debated whether such research would violate Congress's ban on federal funding for research that involves the destruction of human embryos. On January 15, 1999, HHS announced that it would allow federal funding of research on stem cells obtained from human embryos, reasoning that these cells alone are not in themselves embryos. Further congressional debate on this topic is expected.

Tremendous fanfare has greeted the announcement of success in identifying human embryonic stem cells. Fanfare is becoming an increasingly common phenomenon in the world of science and biomedical news. So there is a tendency to greet each week's "breakthrough" with some cynicism. But in the case of the isolation of pluripotent embryonic stem cells the acclaim is surely merited.

Why Is Stem Cell Research So Important?

The identification of human embryonic stem cells has been widely acknowledged as of inestimable value because it will help scientists understand basic mechanisms of embryo development and gene regulation. It also holds the promise of allowing the development of techniques for manipulating, growing and cloning these cells to permit the creation of designer cells and tissues. The availability of immortal stem cell lines will greatly aid drug discovery. The study of stem cells should also shed light on the process of human fertility and

Excerpted from Arthur Caplan's testimony before the U.S. Senate Committee on Appropriations, Subcommittee on Labor, Health and Human Services, and Education, December 2, 1998.

growth and should even open the door to techniques that could be used, some-day, to permit many forms of genetic engineering and transplant therapy for human beings.

There are many in the biomedical community who, when confronting such powerful and useful possibilities, maintain that no steps or actions should be taken to restrict, control, much less prohibit this important research from moving forward. There is even the suggestion that anyone who raises questions about the ethics of human embryo stem cell research is merely using the prospect of research in this area for "political" purposes.

> *"While it is true as a matter of historical fact that all human life has begun with conception it is not true that all conception is capable of becoming human life."*

Such objections are rhetorically powerful but not at all persuasive. As many scientists, policy makers, religious leaders and the American people have long understood, research that may lead to the elucidation of the secrets of human reproduction and development, the modification of the genetic makeup of future children and their children, the creation of new forms of life and a bounty of therapies that hold out the prospect of a longer and better life raises issues of ethics and social policy that must be discussed and debated publicly. It is very appropriate that these issues be raised and examined since human embryonic stem cell research is in its infancy and there is still time to shape and direct its course.

Ethical Concerns Must Be Addressed

Ironically, much of the work being done on human embryonic stem cells is being done without the support of funding from American governmental agencies. This is entirely due to ethical concerns about any research involving human embryos and tissues derived from elective abortions. Embryonic stem cell research has and may involve these sources.

Many worry that to raise any questions about the ethics of stem cell research is to sacrifice a crucially important and incalculably valuable area of biomedical research on the altar of the abortion controversy. They also despair that any dialogue can occur in our society about the ethics of using materials derived or created from embryonic sources given the horrid track record of social divisiveness and violence that are the constant companions of any discussion of abortion in this country.

But the reality is that unless some effort is made to address head on the moral and social issues that embryo stem cell research raises it is very likely that further advances in this area will be slowed as a result of a lack of government support or because they will be conducted completely under private auspices with little accountability and relatively little accessibility to the community of biomedical science. The value of embryonic stem cell research is simply too great to permit a policy stance of inaction to be the response that our government and other governments around the world offer to this enormously promising domain of inquiry. . . .

Not All Embryos Are Created Equally

Most human embryos at the point of conception will not become human beings even under the best of all possible developmental circumstances. Those who study the problem of infertility are beginning to understand what it is about certain eggs and embryos that make them unlikely or unable to develop into fetuses and later babies. While it is true as a matter of historical fact that all human life has begun with conception it is not true that all conception is capable of becoming human life. Nor will it be true for long that all human life must begin with conception. These changing realities mean that a much more fine-tuned and nuanced conceptual framework is needed to keep pace with advances in knowledge and manipulability of human gametes and embryos.

The moral problems with making embryos for research are that as a society we do not want to see embryos treated as products or mere objects for fear that we will cheapen the value of parenting, risk the commercialization of procreation, and trivialize the act of procreation. Society may or may not agree that a human conceptus is deserving of full ethical standing and respect on a par with an adult human being. But, surely we do have a broad consensus in American society

> *"There would be a moral problem if embryos were created solely for the purpose of . . . research. . . . But it is very simple to prevent such practices from occurring."*

that the process of creating embryos that have the potential and ability to become human beings requires special status and standing within our law and our culture.

If that is so then the manufacture of embryos for stem cell research with the potential to become persons may be morally suspect because it violates our desire to accord special standing and status to human conception, procreation and sexuality. To do nothing in this area it should be noted is to consign the practice of embryo creation for generating stem cells to the marketplace which is to completely abrogate any special standing or status to human conception and procreation.

Spare Embryos

One of the greatest ironies of current policies governing embryo research in the United States is that it has created a situation in which a huge industry has arisen to treat infertility with relatively little oversight and accountability for its practices. It has also created a situation in which the demand for clinical services is high but the knowledge base of those providing techniques such as in vitro fertilization (IVF) is not what it might be because of the lack of federal funds to support fundamental research. As a result, when couples seek to use IVF they are required to create more embryos then they or their doctors might wish in order to minimize the need to create more should they fail to have a child and to help insure that at least some embryos will be made that are capable of growth and development. This means that some fortunate couples are lucky enough to have the technique work on a first or second try but wind up with the problem of what to do with remaining surplus or spare embryos. This country now finds itself in a situation in which tens of thousands of orphan embryos sit in liquid nitrogen unwanted and highly unlikely to be used by anyone ever to try to make babies.

Recently the United Kingdom enacted legislation to permit the destruction of unclaimed and unwanted embryos. The United States has not done so but there are thousands of embryos that might be made available for research and study for many purposes including stem cell research if those who created them were given this option or if clinics could make them available for this purpose after a waiting period of say ten years.

Objections to Using Embryos for Research

There are some who would still object that these frozen embryos are still potential persons. But that claim does not square with the facts. If no woman is willing to have the embryos placed inside her bodies, if clinics are reluctant to use embryos that have been stored for long periods of time because their potential to become babies is diminished or if couples do not want anyone else using their embryos then their potential for becoming persons is zero.

There would be a moral problem if embryos were created solely for the purpose of being frozen and then used for research. Such a practice would demean human reproduction and sexuality in turning it into a process of manufacture and mass production. But it is very simple to prevent such practices from occurring. If infertility clinic personnel understood that it was illegal and punishable by fine and prison to inquire if a couple or a woman wanted to freeze embryos until an IVF cycle had been completed, then there would be no incentive to create embryos. Spare, unwanted or damaged embryos could then be made available for stem cell research, storage with consent or future utilization.

"Stem cell research will proceed even without federal funding."

To those who say this is still permitting the use of human embryos for a purpose that is disrespectful, research and the consequent destruction of the embryo, it seems appropriate to ask why continued freezing is not just as disrespectful. It is also appropriate to ask why, even if regrettable and sad, it would not be worth permitting the donation of spare embryos for research that might lead to cures and benefits in much the same way that we allow families to donate their loved ones' organs and tissues under the most tragic of circumstances to aid others? Spare embryos would seem to be a legitimate and morally defensible source of human embryonic stem cells. . . .

Some Possible Moral Principles to Guide Stem Cell Research

It might be helpful once it is recognized that there are no hard and fast lines to be drawn with respect to the ethics of stem cell research to try and advance some simple moral principles that might help those charged with controlling or approving such research. I would suggest the following as principles which are in evidence already in other areas of biomedical research and therapy;

- Seek to achieve the most good or benefit with the least harm and destruction of things of value.
- Tradeoffs to achieve progress in the struggle against disease and disability are both inevitable and ethical.
- The creation of materials with the capacity to become human life is a process that requires moral guidance and humility.
- The complexity of the tradeoffs involved when research is being conducted at the boundaries of human life requires accountability and publicity.

Each of these principles is used to justify activity in biomedical research and therapy that is known to be risky or even known to be harmful but which has important benefits to individuals and society. Our society is quite familiar with the concept of tradeoffs. Americans recognize few moral absolutes and in the area of stem cell research where the tradeoffs frequently involve the possibility of harm to potential persons versus the reality of harm to real flesh and blood persons it is hard not to use some of these principles to guide prudent choices, albeit tragic ones. To be blunt it would be hard to honor principles such as these and the role they play in biomedicine and many areas of public life and still tell the persons paralyzed in a wheelchair or immobile as a consequence of ALS [Lou Gehrig's disease] or Muscular Dystrophy or Parkinson's that they must remain in such states because of inviolate moral concern for the moral standing of an unwanted frozen embryo.

Public Versus Privately Sponsored Research

Perhaps the most neglected factor in weighing what to do with respect to stem cell research is the reality that stem cell research will proceed even without federal funding. It will proceed more slowly, but it will proceed. It will proceed with no accountability, but it will proceed. It will proceed cloaked in secrecy, but it will proceed. And it will proceed with an eye toward the commercially attractive rather than basic knowledge or the public good, but it will proceed. The importance of the benefits to be garnered in this area makes it imperative that speed, accountability, publicity, and the drive to understand shape as much of the early course of stem cell research as is possible. Add to this the fact that the world of embryo sources and the status of stem cells themselves is complex and it becomes certain that it would be better to see publicly sponsored research complement private activities and publicly accountable oversight accompany the market ethos that soon will prevail in the United States if no action is taken by government. . . .

In order to understand what is and is not ethical with respect to stem cell research it is necessary to know a great deal about the nature of the human embryo where such cells must be identified and isolated, something about the stem cells themselves, something about the aims and goals of the research and something about the benefits that are likely to eventuate from a particular research study. Simple moral schemes of classification are not sufficient for negotiating this dense biological terrain. It will take a committee or commission with the time and expertise to review particular proposals from specific researchers to make the judgements that are required.

> *"America needs to seek to allow the many benefits of stem cell research to be secured."*

What Should Be Done?

I conclude with three recommendations based on my understanding of the nature of the issues raised by stem cell research and the complexity of ethical and social questions such research raises:

1. America needs to create a public forum where advances in biology and genetics can be discussed by ethicists, philosophers, theologians and other humanists and social thinkers so as to permit a richer set of concepts and categories to emerge so as to enhance public and political understanding of what it is to talk of the creation of human life, new forms of life and potential life.

2. America needs to seek to allow the many benefits of stem cell research to be secured. This does not, however, make moral discussion of how to proceed simply political. Nor does it mean that concerns and worries about the moral licitness of stem cell and embryo research must always yield to the promise of benefits and new knowledge.

3. America needs to create an oversight body, committee or commission with appropriate expertise to consider and approve requests for research protocols involving stem cell and embryo research.

Research into Human Cloning Should Be Banned

by William Keeler

About the author: **About the author:** *Cardinal William Keeler is archbishop of Baltimore and a member of the National Conference of Catholic Bishops Pro-Life Activities Committee.*

The sanctity and dignity of human life is a cornerstone of Catholic moral reflection and social teaching. We believe a society can be judged by the respect it shows for human life, especially in its most vulnerable stages and conditions.

On this basis the Catholic Church strongly opposes the taking of human life through abortion, euthanasia or destructive experiments on human embryos.

Making Procreation into Manufacture

At first glance, human cloning may not seem to belong on this list. It is presented as a means for creating life, not destroying it. Yet it shows disrespect toward human life in the very act of generating it. Cloning completely divorces human reproduction from the context of a loving union between man and woman, producing children with no "parents" in the ordinary sense. Here human life does not arise from an act of love, but is manufactured to predetermined specifications. A developing human being is treated as an object, not as an individual with his or her own identity and rights. As one group of scientific and other experts advising the Holy See has written:

> In the cloning process the basic relationships of the human person are perverted: filiation, consanguinity, kinship, parenthood. A woman can be the twin sister of her mother, lack a biological father and be the daughter of her grandmother. In vitro fertilization has already led to the confusion of parentage, but cloning will mean the radical rupture of these bonds.

Such moral concern transcends denominational bounds and has been eloquently expressed by some of our country's most respected philosophers and ethicists. Writes Professor Leon Kass of the University of Chicago:

Reprinted from William Keeler's testimony before the U.S. House of Representatives Committee on Commerce, Subcommittee on Health and Environment, February 12, 1998.

Human cloning would . . . represent a giant step toward turning begetting into making, procreation into manufacture (literally, something *handmade*). . . . We here would be taking a major step into making man himself simply another one of the man-made things.

"Second-Class" Human Beings

From the dehumanizing nature of this technique flow many disturbing consequences. Because human clones are produced by a means more suited to more primitive forms of life—a means which involves no loving relationship, no personal investment or responsibility for a new life but only laboratory technique—they would be uniquely at risk of being treated as "second-class" human beings.

The very scenarios often cited as justifications for human cloning are actually symptoms of the moral problem it creates. It has been said that cloning could be used to create "copies" of illustrious people, or to replace a deceased loved one, or even to provide a source of spare tissues or organs for the person whose genetic material was used for the procedure. In each proposal we see a utilitarian view of human life in which a human being is treated as a means to someone else's ends instead of as a person with his or her own inherent dignity. This same attitude lies at the root of human slavery.

Let me be perfectly clear. In reality a cloned human being would not be in any sense an "object" or a substandard human being. Whatever the circumstances of his or her origin, he or she deserves to be treated as a human person with an individual identity. But the depersonalized technique of manufacture known as cloning disregards this dignity and

> *"Cloning is not wrong because cloned human beings lack human dignity— it is wrong because they* have *human dignity."*

sets the stage for further exploitation. Cloning is not wrong because cloned human beings lack human dignity—it is wrong because they *have* human dignity and deserve to come into the world in ways that respect this dignity. Each child has a right to be conceived and born as the fruit of a loving union between husband and wife, to be loved and accepted as a new and distinct individual.

Research Using Cloned Embryos

Ironically, the most startling evidence of the dehumanizing aspects of cloning is found in some proposals ostensibly aimed at preventing human cloning. The National Bioethics Advisory Commission and now some members of Congress favor legislation that would not ban human cloning at all—but would simply ban any effort to allow cloned human beings to survive. In these proposals researchers are allowed to use cloning for the unlimited mass production of human embryos for experimentation—after which they are required to destroy them instead of allowing them to implant in a woman's womb.

Enactment of such a proposal would mark the first time in history that the U.S. government defined a class of human beings that it is a crime *not* to destroy. These human embryos—produced without true parents and hence without protectors—would be created at the outset for the sole purpose of experimentation and destruction.

> *"People somehow assume that a brief life as an object of research, followed by destruction, is 'good enough' for any human produced by [cloning]."*

Human embryo research has been debated in this body before. Three years ago the National Institutes of Health (NIH) proposed that federally funded researchers be allowed to perform nontherapeutic experiments on human embryos produced by in vitro fertilization—including embryos produced solely for research purposes. The moral outcry against this proposal was almost universal. Opinion polls showed massive opposition, and the National Institutes of Health panel making the recommendation was inundated with over 50,000 letters of protest. The *Washington Post*, while reaffirming its stand in favor of legalized abortion, editorialized against the panel's recommendation:

> The creation of human embryos specifically for research that will destroy them is unconscionable. . . . It is not necessary to be against abortion rights or to believe human life literally begins at conception to be deeply alarmed by the notion of scientists purposely causing conceptions in a context entirely divorced from even the potential of reproduction.

President Bill Clinton ultimately set aside the recommendation allowing creation of "research embryos," and since 1995 Congress has voted to prohibit funding of all harmful embryo research—most especially the creation of research embryos.

Morally Irresponsible Policies

Why then are these moral judgments suddenly reversed if the human embryo has been produced by cloning? Why is Congress now being urged to endorse the proposition: "The creation of human embryos by cloning specifically for research that will destroy them is a national priority"? It seems the cloning procedure is so demeaning that people somehow assume that a brief life as an object of research, followed by destruction, is "good enough" for any human produced by this technique. The fact that the procedure invites such morally irresponsible policies is reason enough to oppose it.

The National Bioethics Advisory Commission (NBAC) approach does not even make sense as a barrier to cloning for reproductive purposes. For a great deal of destructive experimentation using cloned human embryos would be a necessary step toward the production of a live-born infant by cloning. We have all learned that as many as 276 sheep embryos, fetuses and newborn lambs had to die so that one sheep, "Dolly," could be produced. Scientists can expect similar results from initial attempts at human cloning—indicating that it would be morally irresponsible to make the attempt. Yet legislation based on the NBAC approach would give the federal government's blessing to such experiments. Researchers who discard hundreds or thousands of human embryos in failed cloning attempts could resort to the defense that such cavalier disposal of human life is exactly what the federal law requires.

Some will ask, by speaking here of a human embryo, let alone a human life, do we inject religious belief into this debate? The answer is emphatically no. Even the NIH Human Embryo Research Panel, which recommended federal funding for destructive human embryo experiments, called the early human embryo "a developing form of human life" which "warrants serious moral consideration." If some wish to deny membership in the human family to human beings in the earliest stage of their development, it is they who impose an ideological filter on the facts. To claim that one is banning "human cloning" by simply banning the nurture or live birth of human embryos already produced by cloning is to distort language and common sense.

The church is also sensitive to claims that cloning is necessary for the pursuit of valuable medical research. We hold that [in the words of Pope John Paul II] "medicine is an eminent, essential form of service to mankind." Research involving the cloning of animals, plants and even human genes, cells and tissues can be beneficial to human beings and presents no intrinsic moral problem. However, when research turns its attention to human subjects, we must be sure that we do not undermine human dignity in the very process of seeking to serve it. Human experimentation divorced from moral considerations may well progress more quickly on a technical level—but at the loss of our sense of humanity. The Tuskegee syphilis study, Nazi Germany's hypothermia experiments and our own government's Cold War radiation experiments will always be remembered in the history of modem medicine—but not in a positive light. Any "progress" thcy may have brought on a technical level is far overshadowed by their mistreatment of human beings.

Research Alternatives

There has been much speculation in recent months about the ways human cloning might revolutionize medical research on various diseases. In all these areas of research, however, alternatives seem to be possible which do not involve the use of cloning technology to create and destroy human embryos. For example, some researchers may want to use somatic-cell nuclear transfer to create "customized stem-cell lines" genetically matched for individual patients—a procedure that in each case would require creating, developing and then killing a human embryo that is the patient's identical twin. Yet even the National

Bioethics Advisory Commission described this avenue of research as "a rather expensive and far-fetched scenario," and reminded us that a moral assessment is necessary as well:

> Because of ethical and moral concerns raised by the use of embryos for research purposes, it would be far more desirable to explore the direct use of human cells of adult origin to produce specialized cells or tissues for transplantation into patients.

Surely, anyone who understands the need for ethically responsible science can agree with this judgment. One great benefit of a ban on human cloning is that it will direct the scientific enterprise toward research that benefits human beings without forcing them to produce, exploit and destroy fellow human beings to gain those benefits. Creating human life solely to cannibalize and destroy it is the most unconscionable use of human cloning—not its highest justification.

Research into Human Cloning Should Not Be Banned

by Ronald Bailey

About the author: *Ronald Bailey is a contributing editor to* Reason, *a monthly magazine of politics and economics.*

By now everyone knows that Scottish biotechnologists have cloned a sheep. They took a cell from a 6-year-old sheep, added its genes to a hollowed-out egg from another sheep, and placed it in the womb of yet another sheep, resulting in the birth of an identical twin sheep that is six years younger than its sister. This event was quickly followed up by the announcement that some Oregon scientists had cloned monkeys. The researchers say that in principle it should be possible to clone humans. That prospect has apparently frightened a lot of people, and quite a few of them are calling for regulators to ban cloning since we cannot predict what the consequences of it will be.

The Rush to Ban Human Cloning

President Bill Clinton rushed to ban federal funding of human cloning research and asked privately funded researchers to stop such research at least until the National Bioethics Advisory Commission issues a report on the ethical implications of human cloning. The commission, composed of scientists, lawyers, and ethicists, was appointed in 1996 to advise the federal government on the ethical questions posed by biotechnology research and new medical therapies. Its report was due in June 1997. [In June 1997, the commission recommended that the moratorium on human cloning be continued for three to five years, and President Clinton instituted a five-year ban.]

But Senator Christopher Bond (R-Mo.) isn't waiting around for the commission's recommendations; he's already made up his mind. Bond introduced a bill to ban the federal funding of human cloning or human cloning research. "I want to send a clear signal," said the senator, "that this is something we cannot and should not tolerate. This type of research on humans is morally reprehensible."

Carl Feldbaum, president of the Biotechnology Industry Organization, hurriedly said that human cloning should be immediately banned. Perennial Luddite Jeremy Rifkin grandly pronounced that cloning "throws every convention, every historical tradition, up for grabs." At the putative opposite end of the political spectrum, conservative columnist George Will

> *"You'd think it was crystal clear why cloning humans is unethical. But what exactly is wrong with it? Which ethical principle does cloning violate?"*

chimed in: "What if the great given—a human being is a product of the union of a man and woman—is no longer a given?"

In addition to these pundits and politicians, a whole raft of bioethicists declared that they, too, oppose human cloning. Daniel Callahan of the Hastings Center said flat out: "The message must be simple and decisive: The human species doesn't need cloning." George Annas of Boston University agreed: "Most people who have thought about this believe it is not a reasonable use and should not be allowed. . . . This is not a case of scientific freedom vs. the regulators."

What Is Wrong with Cloning People?

Given all of the brouhaha, you'd think it was crystal clear why cloning humans is unethical. But what exactly is wrong with it? Which ethical principle does cloning violate? Stealing? Lying? Coveting? Murdering? What? Most of the arguments against cloning amount to little more than a reformulation of the old familiar refrain of Luddites everywhere: "If God had meant for man to fly, he would have given us wings. And if God had meant for man to clone, he would have given us spores." Ethical reasoning requires more than that.

What would a clone be? Well, he or she would be a complete human being who happens to share the same genes with another person. Today, we call such people identical twins. To my knowledge no one has argued that twins are immoral. Of course, cloned twins would not be the same age. But it is hard to see why this age difference might present an ethical problem—or give clones a different moral status.

"You should treat all clones like you would treat all monozygous [identical] twins or triplets," concludes Dr. H. Tristam Engelhardt, a professor of medicine at Baylor and a philosopher at Rice University. "That's it." It would be unethical to treat a human clone as anything other than a human being. If this principle is observed, he argues, all the other "ethical" problems for a secular society essentially disappear. John Fletcher, a professor of biomedical ethics in the medical school at the University of Virginia, agrees: "I don't believe that there is any intrinsic reason why cloning should not be done."

Let's take a look at a few of the scenarios that opponents of human cloning have sketched out. Some argue that clones would undermine the uniqueness of each human being. "Can individuality, identity and dignity be severed from genetic distinctiveness, and from belief in a person's open future?"asks George Will.

Will and others have apparently fallen under the sway of what Fletcher calls "genetic essentialism." Fletcher says polls indicate that some 30 percent to 40 percent of Americans are genetic essentialists, who believe that genes almost completely determine who a person is. But a person who is a clone would live in a very different world from that of his genetic predecessor. With greatly divergent expcriences, their brains would be wired differently. After all, even twins who grow up together are separate people—distinct individuals with different personalities and certainly no lack of Will's "individuality, identity and dignity."

In addition, a clone that grew from one person's DNA inserted in another person's host egg would pick up "maternal factors" from the proteins in that egg, altering its development. Physiological differences between the womb of the original and host mothers could also affect the clone's development. In no sense, therefore, would or could a clone be a "carbon copy" of his or her predecessor.

What about a rich jerk who is so narcissistic that he wants to clone himself so that he can give all his wealth to himself? First, he will fail. His clone is simply not the same person that he is. The clone may be a jerk too, but he will be his own individual jerk. Nor is Jerk Sr.'s action unprecedented.

> *"There's no reason to think that a law against cloning would make much difference anyway."*

Today, rich people, and regular people too, make an effort to pass along some wealth to their children when they die. People will their estates to their children not only because they are connected by bonds of love but also because they have genetic ties. The principle is no different for clones.

Clones Are People

Senator Bond and others worry about a gory scenario in which clones would be created to provide spare parts, such as organs that would not be rejected by the predecessor's immune system. "The creation of a human being should not be for spare parts or as a replacement," says Bond. I agree. The simple response to this scenario is: Clones are people. You must treat them like people. We don't forcibly take organs from one twin and give them to the other. Why would we do that in the case of clones?

The technology of cloning may well allow biotechnologists to develop animals which will grow human-compatible organs for transplant. Cloning is likely to be first used to create animals that produce valuable therapeutic hormones, enzymes, and proteins.

But what about cloning exceptional human beings? George Will put it this way: "Suppose a cloned Michael Jordan, age 8, preferred violin to basketball? Is it imaginable? If so, would it be tolerable to the cloner?" Yes, it is imaginable, and the cloner would just have to put up with violin recitals. Kids are not commercial property—slavery was abolished some time ago. We all know about Little League fathers and stage mothers who push their kids, but given the stubborn nature of individuals, those parents rarely manage to make kids stick forever to something they hate. A ban on cloning wouldn't abolish pushy parents.

One putatively scientific argument against cloning has been raised. As a National Public Radio commentator who opposes cloning quipped, "Diversity isn't just politically correct, it's good science." Sexual reproduction seems to have evolved for the purpose of staying ahead of ever-mutating pathogens in a continuing arms race. Novel combinations of genes created through sexual reproduction help immune systems devise defenses against rapidly evolving germs, viruses, and parasites. The argument against cloning says that if enough human beings were cloned, pathogens would likely adapt and begin to get the upper hand, causing widespread disease. The analogy often cited is what happens when a lot of farmers all adopt the same corn hybrid. If the hybrid is highly susceptible to a particular bug, then the crop fails.

That warning may have some validity for cloned livestock, which may well have to live in environments protected from infectious disease. But it is unlikely that there will be millions of clones of one person. Genomic diversity would still be the rule for humanity. There might be more identical twins, triplets, etc., but unless there are millions of clones of one person, raging epidemics sweeping through hordes of human beings with identical genomes seem very unlikely.

But even if some day millions of clones of one person existed, who is to say that novel technologies wouldn't by then be able to control human pathogens? After all, it wasn't genetic diversity that caused typhoid, typhus, polio, or measles to all but disappear in the United States. It was modern sanitation and modern medicine.

Cloning Is Not Ban-Able

There's no reason to think that a law against cloning would make much difference anyway. "It's such a simple technology, it won't be ban-able," says Engelhardt. "That's why God made offshore islands, so that anybody who wants to do it can have it done." Cloning would simply go underground and be practiced without legal oversight. This means that people who turned to cloning would not have recourse to the law to enforce contracts, ensure proper standards, and hold practitioners liable for malpractice.

Who is likely to be making the decisions about whether human cloning should be banned? When President Clinton appointed the National Bioethics Advisory Commission in 1996, his stated hope was that such a commission could come up with some sort of societal consensus about what we should do with cloning.

The problem with achieving and imposing such a consensus is that Americans live in a large number of disparate moral communities. "If you call up the Pope in Rome, do you think he'll hesitate?"asks Engelhardt. "He'll say, 'No, that's not the way that Christians reproduce.' And if you live Christianity of a Roman Catholic sort, that'll be a good enough answer. And if you're fully secular, it won't be a relevant answer at all. And if you're in-between, you'll feel kind of generally guilty."

Overly Powerful Bioethicists

Engelhardt questions the efficacy of such commissions:

> Understand why all such commissions are frauds. Imagine a commission that really represented our political and moral diversity. It would have as its members Jesse Jackson, Jesse Helms, Mother Teresa, Bella Abzug, Phyllis Schafly. And they would all talk together, and they would never agree on anything. Presidents and Congresses rig—manufacture fraudulently—a consensus by choosing people to serve on such commissions who already more or less agree. . . . Commissions are created to manufacture the fraudulent view that we have a consensus.

Unlike Engelhardt, Fletcher believes that the National Bioethics Advisory Commission can be useful, but he acknowledges that "all of the commissions in the past have made recommendations that have had their effects in federal regulations. So they are a source eventually of regulations." The bioethics field is littered with ill-advised bans, starting in the mid-1970s with the two-year moratorium on recombining DNA and including the law against selling organs and blood and Clinton's recent prohibition on using human embryos in federally funded medical research.

"Bioethicists should have no ability to stop individuals from making their own decisions."

As history shows, many bioethicists succumb to the thrill of exercising power by saying no. Simply leaving people free to make their own mistakes will get a bio-ethicist no perks, no conferences, and no power. Bioethicists aren't the ones suffering, the ones dying, and the ones who are infertile, so they do not bear the consequences of their bans. There certainly is a role for bioethicists as advisers, explaining to individuals what the ramifications of their decisions might be. But bioethicists should have no ability to stop individuals from making their own decisions, once they feel that they have enough information.

Cloning Is Like Any Other Technology

Ultimately, biotechnology is no different from any other technology—humans must be allowed to experiment with it in order to find its best uses and, yes, to make and learn from mistakes in using it. Trying to decide in advance how a technology should be used is futile. The smartest commission ever assembled simply doesn't have the creativity of millions of human beings trying to live the best lives that they can by trying out and developing new technologies.

So why is the impulse to ban cloning so strong? "We haven't gotten over the nostalgia for the Inquisition," concludes Engelhardt. "We are people who are postmodernist with a nostalgia for the Middle Ages. We still want the state to have the power of the Inquisition to enforce good public morals on everyone, whether they want it or not."

Bibliography

Books

John D. Arras and Bonnie Steinbock	*Ethical Issues in Modern Medicine*. Mountain View, CA: Mayfield, 1995.
Patricia Boling, ed.	*Expecting Trouble: Surrogacy, Fetal Abuse, and New Reproductive Technologies*. Boulder, CO: Westview Press, 1995.
Arthur Caplan, Robert M. Veatch, and David H. Smith, eds.	*Am I My Brother's Keeper?: The Ethical Frontiers of Biomedicine*. Bloomington: Indiana University Press, 1998.
Arthur Caplan	*Moral Matters: Ethical Issues in Medicine and the Life Sciences*. New York: John Wiley & Sons, 1995.
Richard J. Devine	*Good Care, Painful Choices: Medical Ethics for Ordinary People*. New York: Paulist Press, 1996.
E. Richard Gold	*Body Parts: Property Rights and the Ownership of Human Biological Materials*. Washington, DC: Georgetown University Press, 1996.
Herbert Hendin	*Seduced by Death: Doctors, Patients, and the Dutch Cure*. New York: W.W. Norton, 1998.
James M. Humber and Robert F. Almeder	*Alternative Medicine and Ethics*. Totowa, NJ: Humana Press, 1998.
Derek Humphry and Mary Clement	*Freedom to Die: People, Politics, and the Right-to-Die Movement*. New York: St. Martin's Press, 1998.
John F. Kilner, Rebecca D. Pentz, and Frank E. Young	*Genetic Ethics: Do the Ends Justify the Genes?* Grand Rapids, MI: William B. Eerdmans, 1997.
Andrew Kimbrell	*The Human Body Shop: The Engineering and Marketing of Life*. Washington, DC: Regnery, 1998.
Gina Kolata	*Clone: The Road to Dolly and the Path Ahead*. New York: William Morrow, 1998.
David Lamb	*Organ Transplants and Ethics*. Brookfield, VT: Avebury, 1996.

Bibliography

Elizabeth L. Marshall *Conquering Infertility: Medical Challenges and Moral Dilemmas*. New York: Watts, 1997.

Gary E. McCuen, ed. *Human Experimentation: When Research Is Evil*. Hudson, WI: Gem, 1998.

Martha Nussbaum and Cass Sunstein, eds. *Clones and Clones: Facts and Fantasies about Human Cloning*. New York: W.W. Norton, 1997.

Patricia and Arthur Parsons *Hippocrates Now! Is Your Doctor Ethical?* Toronto: University of Toronto Press, 1995.

Gregory E. Pence, ed. *Flesh of My Flesh: The Ethics of Cloning Humans: A Reader*. Lanham, MD: Rowman & Littlefield, 1998.

Timothy E. Quill *Death and Dignity: Making Choices and Taking Charge*. New York: W.W. Norton, 1993.

John Rogers, ed. *Medical Ethics, Human Choices: A Christian Perspective*. Scottdale, PA: Herald Press, 1998.

Wesley J. Smith *Forced Exit: The Slippery Slope from Assisted Suicide to Legalized Murder*. New York: Times Books, 1997.

Periodicals

Marcia Angell "The Supreme Court and Physician-Assisted Suicide—The Ultimate Right," *New England Journal of Medicine*, January 2, 1997. Available from 10 Shattuck St., Boston, MA 02115-6094 or www.nejm.org.

AV Magazine "Xenotransplantation and Primates: Threats Masquerading as Cures," Fall 1996. Available from 801 Old York Rd. #204, Jenkintown, PA 19046-1685 or www.aavs.org.

Shannon Brownlee and Joannie M. Schrof "Heartbeats in a Dish," *U.S. News & World Report*, November 16, 1998.

Charles D. Carlstrom and Christy D. Rollow "The Rationing of Organ Transplants: A Troubled Lineup," *Cato Journal*, Fall 1997. Available from the Cato Institute, 1000 Massachusetts Ave. NW, Washington, D.C. 20001-5403 or www.cato.org.

Steven Alan Edwards "Pork Liver, Anyone?" *Technology Review*, July 1996.

Mark D. Eibert "Clone Wars," *Reason*, June 1998.

Ezekiel J. Emanuel "Whose Right to Die?" *Atlantic Monthly*, March 1997.

Josh Fischman "How to Build a Body Part," *Time*, March 1, 1999.

Jeff Goldberg "Fetal Attraction," *Discover*, July 1995.

Toni Gerber Hope "The Ultimate Fertility Guide," *Redbook*, November 1998.

Walter Isaacson "The Biotech Century," special section, *Time*, January 11, 1999.

Issues and Controversies On File "Organ Allocation," May 16, 1997.

Issues and Controversies On File	"Reproductive Technology," April 3, 1998.
Leon R. Kass	"The Wisdom of Repugnance: Why We Should Ban the Cloning of Humans," *New Republic*, June 2, 1997.
Leon R. Kass and Nelson Lund	"Courting Death: Assisted Suicide, Doctors, and the Law," *Commentary*, December 1996.
Charles Krauthammer	"Of Headless Mice . . . and Men: The Ultimate Cloning Horror: Human Organ Farms," *Time*, January 19, 1998.
Michael D. Lemonick	"The New Revolution in Making Babies," *Time*, December 1, 1997.
Gilbert Meilaender	"Biotech Babies: How Far Should Christian Couples Go in the Quest for a Child of Their Own?" *Christianity Today*, December 7, 1998.
Jonathan D. Moreno	"The Dilemmas of Experimenting on People," *Technology Review*, July 1997.
Mother Jones	Special biotechnology report, May/June 1998.
J. Madeleine Nash	"The Age of Cloning," *Time*, March 10, 1997.
Dorothy Nelkin and Lori Andrews	"*Homo Economicus*: Commercialization of Body Tissue in the Age of Biotechnology," *Hastings Center Report*, September/October 1998.
Stephen G. Post	"The Judeo-Christian Case Against Human Cloning," *America*, June 21, 1997.
Susan Reed	"Toward Remedying the Organ Shortage," *Technology Review*, January 1994.
Scientific American	"The Benefits and Ethics of Animal Research," special section, February 1997.
Ruth Shalit	"When We Were Philosopher Kings: The Rise of the Medical Ethicist," *New Republic*, April 28, 1997.
David Shenk	"Biocapitalism: What Price the Genetic Revolution?" *Harper's*, December 1997.
Sheryl Stolberg	"Pennsylvania Set to Break Taboo on Reward for Organ Donations," *New York Times*, May 6, 1999.
Time	Special issue on the frontiers of medicine, Fall 1996.
Meredith Wadman	"Embryo Research Is Pro-Life," *New York Times*, February 21, 1996.
Robert J. White	"Human Embryo Research," *America*, September 14, 1996.
Ian Wilmut	"Cloning for Medicine," *Scientific American*, December 1998.
Chris Wood	"Beyond Abortion," *Maclean's*, August 19, 1996.
Karen Wright	"The Body Bazaar," *Discover*, October 1998.

Organizations to Contact

The editors have compiled the following list of organizations concerned with the issues debated in this book. The descriptions are derived from materials provided by the organizations. All have publications or information available for interested readers. The list was compiled on the date of publication of the present volume; the information provided here may change. Be aware that many organizations take several weeks or longer to respond to inquiries, so allow as much time as possible.

American Life League (ALL)
PO Box 1350, Stafford, VA 22555
(540) 659-4171 • fax: (540) 659-2586
e-mail: whylife@all.org • website: http://www.all.org

ALL is an educational pro-life organization that opposes abortion, artificial contraception, reproductive technologies, and fetal experimentation. It asserts that it is immoral to perform experiments on living human embryos and fetuses. The American Bioethics Advisory Commission, a division of ALL, addresses issues such as cloning, genetic research, and reproductive technologies. Its publications include *NIH and Human Embryo Research Revisited: What Is Wrong with This Picture?* and *Cloning: When Word Games Kill.*

Americans for Medical Progress (AMP)
421 King St., Suite 401, Alexandria, VA 22314
(703) 836-9595 • fax: (703) 836-9594
e-mail: info@amprogress.org • website: http://www.amprogress.org

Americans for Medical Progress is a nonprofit organization whose mission is to promote a better understanding of the role of animals in medical research. It has published numerous articles, including *The Tragic Hypocrisy of "Animal Rights," Animal Research Saves Human Lives,* and *Nobel Prize Shows Animals Are Vital to Medical Research.*

American Society for Reproductive Medicine (ASRM)
1209 Montgomery Hwy., Birmingham, AL 35216
(205) 978-5000 • fax: (205) 978-5005
e-mail: asrm@asrm.org • website: http://www.asrm.org

Established in 1944, ASRM is a voluntary, nonprofit organization devoted to advancing knowledge and expertise in reproductive medicine and biology. The society publishes reports, booklets, and videos on infertility, and the ASRM Ethics Committee issues policy statements on the responsible use of reproductive technologies.

Center for Bioethics
University of Pennsylvania
3401 Market St. #320, Philadelphia, PA 19104
(215) 898-3453 • fax: (215) 573-3036
website: www.bioethics.net

The Center of Bioethics at the University of Pennsylvania is the largest bioethics center in the world, and it runs the world's first and largest bioethics website. It engages in research in and publishes articles about many areas of bioethics. *PennBioethics* is its quarterly newsletter.

Center for Bioethics and Human Dignity (CBHD)

2065 Half Day Road, Bannockburn, IL 60015
(847) 317-8180 • fax: (847) 317-8153
e-mail: cbhd@biccc.org • website: http://www.bioethix.org

CBHD is an international educational center whose purpose is to bring Christian perspectives to bear on contemporary bioethical challenges facing society. Its publications address such topics as euthanasia, genetic technologies, and abortion. It publishes the newsletter *Dignity* and the book *Genetic Ethics: Do the Ends Justify the Genes?*

Center for Disease Control—Office of Genetics and Disease Prevention (OGDP)

4770 Buford Hwy., Mailstop K28, Atlanta, GA 30341-3724
(770) 488-3235 • fax: (770) 488-3236
e-mail: genetics@cdc.gov • website: http://www.cdc.gov/genetics

The purpose of the Office of Genetics and Disease Prevention is to provide a coordinated focus for CDC-wide, cross-cutting genetics efforts and to raise awareness of genetics and disease prevention. It has published the reports *Ethical and Social Issues in the Use of Biomarkers in Epidemiological Research* and *Informed Consent for Stored Tissue Samples.*

Christian Medical and Dental Society (CMDS)

PO Box 7500, 501 5th St., Bristol, TN 37621-7500
(423) 844-1000 • fax: (423) 844-1005
e-mail: main@christian-doctors.com • website: http://www.cmds.org

The CMDS Ethics Commission examines medical ethics issues from a biblical perspective. It supports artificial insemination and in-vitro fertilization in certain cases, as is explained in the society's position paper *Reproductive Technology.* Its publications include the article *The Ethics of Reproductive Technology* and the abstract *Making Babies: The New Technology and the "Old" Morality.*

Citizens United Resisting Euthanasia (CURE)

812 Stephen St., Berkeley Springs, WV 25411
(304) 258-5433 • fax: (304) 258-6420
e-mail: cureltd@ix.netcom.com • website: http://www.netcom.com/~cureltd

CURE is a nationwide coalition of concerned citizens who oppose euthanasia. It works to protect patients and their families against the dangers of involuntary nontreatment. CURE offers extensive literature on euthanasia, including *Brain Death—The Hoax That Won't Die* and its *Life Matters* brochure series.

Compassion in Dying

6312 SW Capitol Hwy, Suite 415, Portland, OR 97201
(503) 221-9556 • fax: (503) 228-9160
e-mail: info@compassionindying.org • website: http://www.compassionindying.org

Compassion in Dying works to provide national leadership for client services, legal advocacy, and public education to improve pain and symptom management, increase patient empowerment and self-determination, and expand end-of-life choices to include aid-in-dying for terminally ill, mentally competent adults.

Department of Health and Human Services Organ Donor Initiative
Health Resources and Services Administration, Division of Transplantation
200 Independence Ave. SW, Washington, DC 20201
(301) 443-7577 • fax: (301) 594-6095
rlaeng@hrsa.gov • website: http://www.organdonor.com

The Department of Health and Human Services is the government's principal agency for protecting the health of all Americans and providing essential human services. The Organ Donor Initiative strives to increase organ and tissue donation. It publishes numerous press releases, fact sheets, and transcripts of Congressional testimony.

The Hastings Center
Route 9D, Garrison, NY 10524-5555
(914) 424-4040 • fax: (914) 424-4545
e-mail: mail@thehastingscenter.org • website: http://www.hastingscenter.org

The Hastings Center is an independent research institute that explores the medical, ethical, and social ramifications of biomedical advances. The center publishes books, papers, guidelines, and the bimonthly *Hastings Center Report*.

The Hemlock Society
PO Box 101810, Denver, CO 80250
(800) 247-7421 • (303) 639-1202 • fax: (303) 639-1224
e-mail: hemlock@privatei.com • website: http://www.hemlock.org/hemlock

The society believes that terminally ill individuals have the right to commit suicide. The society publishes books on suicide, death, and dying, including *Final Exit*, a guide for those suffering with terminal illnesses and considering suicide, and *TimeLines*, the society's quarterly newsletter.

Infertility Awareness Association of Canada (IAAC)
406-One Nicholas St., Ottawa, ON K1N 7B7 CANADA
(613) 244-7222 • fax: (613) 244-7333
e-mail: iaac@fox.nstn.ca • website: http://fox.nstn.ca/~iaac

The Infertility Awareness Association of Canada is a national charitable organization working for choices and access to treatment for those with infertility concerns. IAAC publishes the monthly *Infertility Awareness* newsletter, the quarterly *Canadian Journal of Infertility Awareness*, and the annual *Consumer Journal*.

International Anti-Euthanasia Task Force (IAETF)
PO Box 760, Steubenville, OH 43952
(740) 282-3810
e-mail: info@iaetf.org • website: http://www.iaetf.org

The task force opposes euthanasia, assisted suicide, and policies that threaten the lives of the medically vulnerable. IAETF publishes fact sheets and position papers on euthanasia-related topics in addition to the bimonthly newsletter, *IAETF Update*. It analyzes the policies and legislation concerning medical and social work organizations and files amicus curaie briefs in major "right-to-die" cases.

National Bioethics Advisory Commission (NBAC)
6100 Executive Boulevard, Suite 5B01, Rockville, Maryland 20892-7508
(301) 402-4242 • fax: (301) 480-6900
website: http://www.bioethics.gov

NBAC is a federal agency which sets guidelines that govern the ethical conduct of research. It works to protect the rights and welfare of human research subjects and govern the management and use of genetic information. Its published reports include *Research Involving Persons with Mental Disorders That May Affect Decision-making Capacity* and *Cloning Human Beings.*

National Institutes of Health (NIH)
Health and Human Services Dept., Human Genome Research
9000 Rockville Pike, Bethesda, MD 20892
(301) 402-0911 • fax: (301) 402-0837
e-mail: nihinfo@od.nih.gov • website: http://www.nih.gov

The NIH plans, coordinates, and reviews the progress of the Human Genome Project and works to improve techniques for cloning, storing, and handling DNA. It offers several publications about the Human Genome Project.

Organ Keeper
PO Box 4413, Middletown, RI 02842
e-mail: feedback@organkeeper.com • website: http://www.organkeeper.com

Organ Keeper believes the government's organ donation policies have created an organ donor shortage. It promotes market-based alternatives to the current system of procuring and allocating human organs for transplantation.

People for the Ethical Treatment of Animals (PETA)
501 Front St., Norfolk, VA 23510
(757) 622-7382 • fax: (757) 622-0457
e-mail: info@peta-online.org • website: http://www.peta-online.org

PETA is an educational and activist group that opposes all forms of animal exploitation. It conducts rallies and demonstrations to focus attention on animal experimentation, the fur fashion industry, and the killing of animals for human consumption. It publishes reports on animal experimentation and animal farming and periodic *People for the Ethical Treatment of Animals—Action Alerts.*

Physicians Committee for Responsible Medicine (PCRM)
5100 Wisconsin Ave., Suite 404, Washington, DC 20016
(202) 686-2210 • fax: (202) 686-2216
e-mail: pcrm@pcrm.org • website: http://www.pcrm.org

PCRM is a nonprofit organization of physicians that promotes alternatives to animal experimentation and encourages higher standards for ethics and effectiveness in research. PCRM publishes the quarterly magazine *Good Medicine.*

United Network for Organ Sharing (UNOS)
PO Box 13770, Richmond, VA 23225
(804) 330-8500
website: http://www.unos.org

UNOS is a system of transplant and organ procurement centers, tissue-typing labs, and transplant surgical teams. It was formed to help organ donors and people who need organs to find each other. By federal law, organs used for transplants must be cleared through UNOS. The network also formulates and implements national policies on equal access to organs and organ allocation, organ procurement, and AIDS testing. It publishes the monthly *UNOS Update.*

Index

abortion, 34, 70, 106, 121, 136
  destigmatized by embryo research, 145
  of fetuses in multiple pregnancies, 90, 92
  utilitarian definition of life implied by, 131
acute tubular necrosis (ATN), 52
Advanced Cell Technology, 144
Africa, 81
AIDS, 28–29, 63, 64, 70
Alaska, 46
alcohol abuse, 77
Alexian Brothers Hospital, 40
Alzheimer's disease, 73, 74, 144
American Lung Association, 144
American Red Cross, 75
American Society for Reproductive
  Medicine, 90, 91, 94, 95, 102
Americans with Disabilities Act (ADA), 99
Amnesty International, 84
Anderson, W. French, 140
Angell, Marcia, 33
Animal Issues (magazine), 61
Animal Protection Institute (API), 61, 65, 66
Annas, George, 96, 159
Aquinas, Thomas, 138
Archives of Internal Medicine, 48
Arizona State University, 106
Aronson, Diane D., 97
Asia, 80, 81
  see also China; India; Japan
Australia, 95

Baby K, 27–28
Baby M, 92
Baby Ryan, 39
Baby Terry, 38–39
Bailey, Ronald, 158
Baruch College, 95
Belgium, 80, 82, 85
Bellagio Task Force, 85
Bentham, Jeremy, 18
Berg, Doran, 37, 38
Berger, Alan, 61
Beth Israel Deaconess Medical Center, 98,
  99
Bible, 103, 106, 122

  on infertility, 102, 105
  on sacredness of human life, 104
Bielicki v. The City of Chicago, 99
Biotechnology Industry Organization, 159
blood donation, 51, 68, 76, 111, 162
  and exploitation of poor when
    commercialized, 74
  and risk of disease transmission, 75
Bond, Christopher, 158, 160
Boston, 98, 99
Boston University, 96, 159
Bouchard, Thomas, 112
Boys from Brazil, The (film), 109
Bragdon v. Abbott, 99
brain-damaged patients, 36
  withdrawal of life support from, 37
    based on futile-care theory, 38, 40
    is inappropriate, 39, 41
Brave New World (Huxley), 116
Brazil, 54
Brown, Louis, 13, 116, 119
Brown University School of Medicine, 67
Bulgaria, 123

California, 102, 118, 145
  futile-care policies in, 37–38, 39, 40
Callahan, Daniel, 42, 130, 159
Cambodia, 123
Caplan, Arthur, 15, 53, 94, 139, 147
caring approach in medicine, 17
  actions determined by consequences, 18
    and patient choice, 19
  consistent with Hippocratic oath, 26
  versus curing tradition, 20–23
  see also physician-assisted suicide
Case Western Reserve University, 73
Casey, Bob, 56
Catholic Church, 76, 138, 145, 153–57, 162
  position on cloning, 129–31
Center for Biomedical Ethics, 15, 73, 120,
  147
Centers for Disease Control (CDC), 63, 66
children, 125–26
  of assisted reproduction, 95–96, 121–22
  as commodities, 117

cloned, 130–31
and need for loving parents, 111, 121–22, 154
waiting for adoption, 123
China, 76
organ selling in, 14, 80, 81, 85, 86
using organs from executed prisoners, 83–84
Chosen Death: The Dying Confront Assisted Suicide (Shavelson), 31
Chukwu octuplets, 107, 108, 126, 127
expenses of, 98
and problems of premature infants, 124–25
Cleveland Clinic, 77
Clinton, Bill, 94, 155, 158, 161, 162
Clinton administration, 143, 144
Clomid, 89, 90, 107, 127
cloning. *See* Dolly (cloned sheep); human cloning
Code Gray (film), 19–20
Committee on Morals and Ethics of the Transplantation Society, 67
Commonweal (journal), 129
Congress, U.S., 110, 137, 144, 147
harmful embryo research banned by, 155
on human cloning, 154
Craft, Ian, 116, 118
Creutzfeldt-Jakob disease (CJD), 63
Cruzan, Nancy, 36
Cuba, 81
curing tradition in medicine, 17, 25
hope of remedy implied by, 19
occasional futility of, 26
physicians as the primary decision makers in, 18
versus caring approach, 20–23
see also futile-care approach
cyclosporin, 14, 59, 81

Dayton, Lang, 39
death, 42
can be slow and agonizing, 33
and should be assisted if necessary, 34
hastening of, is becoming routine, 36–38
and legal battles being fought over, 39–40
human preference to postpone, 59–60
as natural event, 30, 43–44
and need to accept, 29
no longer a barrier to production of children, 118
seen as defeat by physicians, 20, 24
Death with Dignity National Center, 31
Dellinger, Walter, 46
Department of Health and Human Services (DHHS), 56, 61, 144, 147
Department of Organ Sharing (DOS), 71

depression, 42
diabetes, 66, 73, 134, 144
Dickey, Jay, 137
Discover magazine, 88
doctors
changing role of, 22
commitment to persons, not biological life, 28
death of patients seen as failure by, 20
and expectations of patients, 21
as medical consultants, 18–19
need courage and compassion, 34
need legal freedom to help patients, 35
as paternalistic, 18
and potential conflict of interests with patients, 48
responsibilities of, 13, 17
killing not included among, 43
to relieve suffering, 31
as travel agents for organ seekers, 84
see also curing tradition in medicine; physician-assisted suicide
Doerflinger, Richard, 145
Dolly (cloned sheep), 13, 94, 109, 114, 138
and implications of successful cloning, 129
result of multiple attempts to produce, 156
and stem cell research, 139
Domar, Alice D., 99
Dow Corning, 107
Duke University Medical Center, 141
Dumas, Rhetaugh, 138
du Pont, Pete, 77

Easterbrook, Gregg, 133
Eastman, Ronald, 146
Ebola virus, 55
Edwards, Robert, 96
Egypt, 54
Emanuel, Ezekiel J., 124
Employee Retirement Income Security Act (ERISA), 100
end-stage renal disease (ESRD), 67, 68, 69, 71, 72
Engelhardt, Tristam, 159, 161, 162, 163
European Union, 139

Fagan, John, 145
FBI (Federal Bureau of Investigation), 84
Feldbaum, Carl, 159
Fertility and Sterility, 100
fertility drugs, 88, 89–90, 91, 107
Fertinex, 89, 91
Field, Loren, 136
Final Exit (Humphry), 19
Finn, Hugh, 36, 37, 38
Fletcher, John, 134, 159, 160
Florida, 40, 100

Follistim, 89
Food and Drug Administration, U.S., 64
Forced Exit: The Slippery Slope from
   Assisted Suicide to Legalized Murder
   (Smith), 36
Frankfurter, David, 98
futile-care approach, 29–30, 38
   dangers of, 39, 40, 41
   doctors feel obliged to provide, 24
   doctors not obliged to provide, 27
   includes mechanical respirators, 25
   as waste of resources, 28

gamete intrafallopian transfer (GIFT), 91,
   92, 116, 120
Gearhart, John, 134, 137, 138, 144
   on Down's syndrome, 133
   use of aborted fetuses by, 135, 136
genetic engineering, 140–41, 161
   see also human cloning
Geron, 135, 136, 146
Gilmore, James, 36
Giuliano, Karen K., 51
Graven family, 90–91
Green, Reginald and Maggie, 75
Griffin, Martha, 100
Grifo, Jamie, 93, 94, 95

Harkin, Tom, 137, 143
Harvard University
   Medical School, 67
   School of Public Health, 62
Haseltine, William, 144
Hastings Center, 42
Hawaii, 46
health care system, 46
   economics of, 47–48, 49
   future of, 41
   inequities in, 62–63
   limits of, 42–43
   need for preventive approach in, 65–66
   see also doctors; patients
Hemlock Society, 47
hepatitis, 70, 75, 77
Higgins, Heather, 114
Hippocratic oath, 26, 31, 41
   versus patient autonomy, 17
Hollister, Margaret, 92
homosexuals, 112
Hong Kong, 63, 81, 84, 110
Howard Hughes Medical Center, 145
human cloning, 88, 94, 110
   as asexual reproduction, 118
   and evolution, 113
   infertility not sufficient justification for,
      130–31
   moral/ethical problems with, 13, 115,

129–31
   include risk of producing "second-class"
      humans, 154
   and need for children to have parents,
      111
   and risks versus benefits, 114
   research into
      alternatives to, 156
      moral objections to, 153–57
   rush to ban, 158–59
      is inappropriate, 159–60, 162–63
      is ineffective, 161
   as solution for infertile couples, 112
human embryos, 92, 137
   moral obligation to care for, 120–21
   and religious principles, 104
   research use of, 135–37
      as acceptable, 147–52
      federal funding banned for, 94, 155, 162
      moral problems with, 145
         include marketing of fetal tissue, 73–74
         and potential to treat disease, 134
         as violation of federal ban, 144
   routine freezing of, 116
Human Genome Sciences, 144
Human Rights Watch/Asia, 84
Humegon, 89
Humphry, Derek, 19, 47
Hurley Medical Center, 38
Huxley, Aldous, 116

India, 54, 74, 85
   organ selling in, 76–77, 80, 81, 82–83
Indiana, 100
Indiana University School of Medicine, 58,
   136
infertility, 97
   need for insurance coverage for, 101
influenza, 63, 64
Institute of Cancer Research, 63
International Anti-Euthanasia Task Force, 36
intracytoplasmic sperm injection (ICSI), 95,
   120
in vitro fertilization (IVF), 88, 102, 120, 130
   costs of, 92, 98, 122
      and lack of federal funds for research,
         150
   eggs fertilized outside womb in, 116
   ethical dilemmas of, 92–93, 117, 119
      include disposal of embryos, 135, 137
      include use of corpses, 118
   low success rates of, 91
Iraq, 54

Japan, 54, 76, 84, 110
Jecker, Nancy S., 24
Jenner, Edward, 57

Jennings, Marianne Moody, 106
John Paul II (pope), 156
Johns Hopkins University, 133, 136, 144, 146
Jordan, Michael, 160
Journal of the American Medical Association, 21, 78
Juvenile Diabetes Foundation, 145

Kaiser/Commonwealth Fund, 62
Kass, Leon, 153, 154
Keeler, William, 153
Kevorkian, Jack, 14, 19
King, Stewart A., 31
Kirkland, Peter, 64

Laing, Jacqueline, 116
Lamont, Gil, 61
Legacy Emanuel Children's Hospital, 39
libertarianism, 68, 70, 72, 73, 74
living will, 21, 22
Loma Linda University School of Medicine, 102
Lu, Leonard, 67

mad cow disease (bovine encephalopathy), 63
malpractice insurance, 20, 22
Marcus, Fred S., 31
Marker, Rita L., 45
Markert, Louise, 141
Martin, Michael, 37, 38
Maryland, 65
Massachusetts, 38
McCaughey family, 107, 124, 126, 127
  fertility drugs used by, 89
  multiple birth viewed as positive by, 108
  refusal to abort any fetuses, 90
McConchie, Daniel, 120
McKay, Ron, 134
McNatt, Bob, 38
Medicaid, 28, 46
Medical University of South Carolina, 78
Medicare, 71
Mellert, Robert B., 17
Mercer, William M., 99, 100
Metrodin, 89
Michigan, 38, 100
  Supreme Court, 37
Middle East, 80, 81, 82
Midwife Through the Dying Process, A (Quill), 31
Mill, John Stuart, 26
Miller, John J., 143
Moral Matters: Ethical Issues in Medicine and the Life Sciences (Caplan), 15, 147
Moral Sense, The (Wilson), 109

Morgan, Jim, 65
morphine, 35
multiple pregnancies, 89, 90, 104, 121, 122
  as comparatively rare, 107
  costs of, 126–27
    exaggeration about, 107–108
  hypocrisy of condemning, 106
  need to prevent, 98, 127–28
  problems associated with, 90, 124–26
Munro, Robin, 84

National Abortion and Reproductive Rights Action League, 144
National Bioethics Advisory Commission, 94, 138, 157, 158, 161
  human cloning not completely banned by, 154–55, 156
National Center for Policy Analysis, 77
National Coalition on Health Care, 62
National Conference of Catholic Bishops, 145, 153
National Institute of Medical Research (NIMR), 63, 64
National Institute of Neurological Disorders and Stroke, 134
National Institutes of Health (NIH), 124, 134, 138, 155
  ethics guidelines of, 73, 140–41
    ambiguity of, 144–45
  sale of fetuses forbidden by, 74
National Organ and Tissue Donor Initiative, 65
National Organ Transplant Act, 53, 77
National Osteoporosis Foundation, 144
National Review, 143
Nazi experiments, 156
Netherlands, 42, 45
Network for Organ Sharing, 77
Nevada, 100
New England Journal of Medicine, 33
New Hampshire, 100
New Jersey, 65, 95, 100
Newsweek, 89
New York, 40, 84, 100
  Civil Liberties Union, 144
New York Times, 53, 95, 124, 145
New York University Medical Center, 93
Novartis, 59
Nursing magazine, 51

Okarma, Thomas, 136
Oregon, 14, 39, 45, 46, 158
organ allocation programs, 55–56, 65, 71, 78
  and shortage of organs, 60, 61, 63
organ transplantation, 14, 15, 51, 139
  and commercial approach to finding organs, 73

benefits of, 77, 79
from cloned humans, 110, 111, 160
dangers of, 54, 74–76
   include human rights violations, 83–85
   include lack of international regulation, 80
framework for, 70–72, 78
is ethical, 68–70
laws against, 162
motivations for, 53, 67
physicians should oppose, 85–86
importance of volunteerism in, 75
with organs from patients' relatives, 52
difficulties of, 53
and risks to donors, 52, 53, 54
insignificance of, 68, 69
and ways to minimize, 71, 72
see also organ allocation programs; xenotransplantation
Orthodox Judaism, 76

Panak, William F., 100
Parkinson's disease, 74, 134, 151
paternalism, 79
patients
desires of, sometimes ignored, 21
responsibilities of, 22
right to autonomy, 17, 19, 27
suffering of, may be increased by futile care, 25
Pennsylvania, 65, 100
People magazine, 124
Pergonal, 89
Philippines, 54
physician-assisted suicide, 14, 15, 32
as compassionate, 31
criteria for, 32
as cruel, 49
difficulty of controlling, 45
economic considerations, 47–48
is ethical, 32–33
medical ethics are violated by, 42–44
as patient's choice, 33, 34
patients' need for, exaggerated by publicity stunts, 46
reality of, 34–35
see also brain-damaged patients
pigs, 54
organs of, for humans, 59, 60, 61
viruses may be a problem in, 55, 63–64
Popper, Karl, 26
pornography, 70
Porter, Charles, 65
Post, Stephen G., 73
Presumed Consent Law, 65
Protestantism, 76
Public Health Service, U.S., 55, 64

Quill, Timothy E., 31

Rabb, Harriet S., 144, 145
Radin, Margaret, 83
Reason (magazine), 158
Reproductive Biology Associates, 93
reproductive technologies, 88–92, 94–96
adoption a good alternative to, 123
banned for unmarried people in some countries, 103
Christian beliefs consistent with, 102–105
costs of, 122
dangers of, 95–96
   for children, 95–96
   include multiple births, 98
growth of, 116
lack of control in, 149–50
   and need for regulation, 94–95
low success rates of, 91
as medical treatment, 97, 98
   and need for infertility insurance, 100–101
   valid because infertility is disability, 99
moral problems with, 92–93, 117–19, 120–22
sperm donation, 75, 76, 121, 122
see also fertility drugs; human cloning; in vitro fertilization (IVF)
Resolve—The National Fertility Association, 97
Rifkin, Jeremy, 15, 159
right-to-die movement, 32, 45
Roe v. Wade, 138
Rothman, Barbara Katz, 95
Rothman, Cappy, 118
Rothman, David J., 80
Royce, Josiah, 108
Russia, 70, 81, 85

Sade, Robert M., 78
sanctity of human life, 18
San Francisco, 49
Schneiderman, Lawrence J., 24
Scotland, 13, 129
Seed, Richard, 13, 94
SerVaas, Cory, 57
Shalala, Donna, 145
Shavelson, Lonny J., 31
Singapore, 81, 84
Smith, Austin, 140
Smith, Wesley J., 36, 49
South Africa, 86
South America, 81
Spain, 60
Specter, Arlen, 137, 144, 145, 146
St. Barnabas Medical Center, 95

stem cell research, 143, 156
  connection to human cloning, 141–42
  ethical concerns about, 145, 148–52
    possible moral framework, 151
  moral problems with, 135, 145
    include religious controversy, 138–39
    include use of fetal tissue, 136–37
  potential benefits of, 133–34, 144, 149
    still distant, 146
  significance of, 140
Stoye, Jonathan P., 64
Sumeria, 141
Supreme Court, U.S., 36, 37, 46, 99
  decision against physician-assisted suicide,
    33, 34
  injustice of, 35
surrogate motherhood, 88, 102, 122, 130
  as commercial arrangement, 70, 76
  various forms of, 92–93

Taiwan, 84, 85
Tennessee, 38, 100
Texas, 38, 100
Thomson, James, 133–34, 135, 137, 138,
  144
Thurow, Lester Carl, 69–70
Time (magazine), 89
Titmuss, Richard, 74, 75
Transplant Recipient and Donor
  Organization (TRADO), 78
*Troubled Dream of Life: In Search of a
  Peaceful Death* (Callahan), 42
Turkey, 54, 80
Tuskegee syphilis study, 156

United Kingdom, 54, 57, 63, 137, 150
  sale of organs prohibited in, 67
  shortage of organ donors in, 60
United Network for Organ Sharing, 55, 56,
  61, 82
United States, 60, 81, 139, 150, 152
  commercialization of blood supply in, 74
  embryo research in, 149
    and ban on federal funding, 94
  fertility problems in, 92, 97, 120
    and number of fertility clinics, 89
  increased number of multiple births in, 95
  modern medical advances in, 161
  organ donation legal in, 53
  organ selling banned in, 67, 70
  transplant waiting lists in, 80
  vegetative patients in, 26

University of California
  School of Medicine, 24
  Los Angeles, 109
University of Chicago, 153
University of Edinburgh, 140
University of Michigan, 138
University of Minnesota, 83, 112
University of Pennsylvania, 15, 94
University of Southern California, 140
University of Virginia, 134
University of Washington School of
  Medicine, 24
University of Wisconsin, 133, 144
utilitarianism, 18, 19, 41, 68, 69
  in commodification of human body, 70, 72,
    131

Vacco v. Quill, 33
Varmus, Harold, 134, 138, 144
Vinson, Rebekah, 37
Virginia, 118

Wall Street Journal, 62
Washington Post, 124, 144, 155
Washington state, 39, 77
Washington v. Glucksberg, 33
Wendland, Florence, 37
Wendland, Robert, 37, 38
West, Michael, 144
White, David, 57, 58
Whitney, Elvonne, 102
Wilder, Marcy, 144, 145
Will, George, 159, 160
Williamson, Beverly, 39
Wilmut, Ian, 129, 130, 139
Wilson, James Q., 109
Winston, Robert, 116
Wisconsin, 135
World Medical Association, 85
Wright, Karen, 88

xenotransplantation (use of animal organs
  for humans), 54, 55, 57, 61
  alternatives to, 65–66
  benefits of, 59–60
  dangers of, 63, 64
  expense of, 62
  history of, 58

Younger, Benjamin, 90

zygote intrafallopian transfer (ZIFT), 120